SOCIAL DEMOCRACY IN BRITAIN

Must Labour Lose?

Peter Zentner

SOCIAL DEMOCRACY IN BRITAIN

Must Labour Lose?

John Martin Publishing
London

First published 1982 in Great Britain by
John Martin Publishing Limited
15 King Street, London WC2

ISBN
0 906 237 22 X Hardback
0 906 237 20 3 Paperback

Typeset by John Martin -
Winchmore Press Datalink

Printed and bound in Great Britain by
Short Run Press, Exeter, Devon

To Carola, whose comments and journalistic advice were invaluable, and to my five children, Adam, Laurence, Marcus, Quentin and Vicky, and to Simon.

CONTENTS

PREFACE
INTRODUCTION   1

PART I
PROFILE OF THE SDP AT BIRTH:
THE FIRST WEEKS
  1 SDP — Antidote to Frustration   5
  2 SDP: First Successes   10
  3 SDP: Why No Policies?   16
  4 The Leadership   20

PART II
THE OLD LABOUR PARTY:
SOCIAL DEMOCRATIC HERITAGE
  5 What is Labour? The Sentimental Myth   27
  6 British Socialism — Consensus Style   32
  7 Electoral Defeat 1959: The Seeds of the Future   38
  8 Conference and PLP: Trial Separation 1960-1   46
  9 Campaign for Democratic Socialism:
       Model for the Future   51

PART III
LABOUR PARTY UNDER NEW MANAGEMENT:
SOCIAL DEMOCRACY UNDER PRESSURE
  10 The Wilson Years   59
  11 The Common Market Issue   78
  12 First Attempt at Social Democracy   86
  13 The Frustrated Society   91
  14 The Demoralised Right: Reluctant
       Fellow Travellers of the Seventies   99

PART IV
COUNT-DOWN TO A LABOUR PARTY SPLIT
15 The Make-or-Break Issue: Party Democracy   117
16 1979-81: Steep Road to Limehouse   122

PART V
THE SHOW ON THE ROAD
17 Limehouse to Warrington   151
18 Warrington   166
19 The Liberal Connection   174
20 From Warrington Onwards   183

CONCLUSION
WHAT FUTURE THE PROGRESSIVE LEFT?   191

CHRONOLOGY   209
RESEARCH SOURCES   213
INDEX   219

PREFACE

There can have been few more dramatic happenings in recent British politics than the successful establishment of the Social Democratic Party (SDP). Launched with razzamatazz in March 1981, somewhat to the surprise of the electorate, nine months later it is difficult to imagine a time without it.

But could the new party vanish as rapidly as it emerged, as the electorate increasingly focusses upon the choice of Government at the next General Election, whenever it comes, in 1983 or 1984? The older political parties would wish the SDP to disappear and have predicted its demise: but they have a vested interest in the outcome, of course.

Sudden though this new party's emergence may seem, its roots are deep in our Western political tradition, in particular the traditions of the left. In this book Peter Zentner traces the emergence of the new party over a twenty-year period. His thesis is that the historical evolution of the SDP is also a description of the decline of the Labour Party. He argues that under the British electoral system, so long as the Labour Party prospers, there is no future for any alternative political grouping left of centre.

Must then the success of the SDP signal electoral disaster for the Labour Party? The answer is by no means clear, for even if we accept the thesis of the irreversible decline of the Labour Party, the emergence of the new party means that the winning post has been shifted. The winning share of the votes is dramatically lower in a genuine and tightly fought three-party election. Labour might win a General Election, given our single member, first-past-the-post system of election, on an historically low share of the total votes cast.

Peter Zentner argues cogently that Labour is losing and will lose and that the future of the progressive parliamentary Left lies now with the SDP.

INTRODUCTION

Writing this book has made me relive the political events of the last years. Doing so was a little like seeing an old film. One remembered the atmosphere and the broad outline of the story. The details and individual episodes were forgotten, brought back again by the research and the writing.

In preparing this book, I have kept before me two types of people who might be interested: those who like me have lived through this period and who might wish to recall the excitement of the first post-war Labour administrations and the consequent downhill slide, and those of a younger generation who have no personal experience of those years.

Some younger readers may have viewed the birth of the Social Democratic Party with scepticism, seeing it as the creation of the moment, breathed into life by opportunistic politicians. For them, this book may throw light on social democracy, indicating a longer history and honourable credentials. The SDP was born out of years of conflict, out of a party where moderates were increasingly under attack. In the end, when the SDP emerged as a fledgling party, it was responding not only to internal pressures in the Labour Party but also to the prompting of a waiting electorate. The extraordinary rise of the SDP in its first year is proof that it is not opportunism which brought it into existence, but the electorate itself.

There were many people like myself who, over the last decade, had felt disenfranchised. Ever since the Labour Party started to stray from the straight path of principles, to take the winding road of expediency in a spirit of acrimony rather than tolerance, support had ebbed. People stopped voting for Labour for different reasons at different times but the recorded figures of decline are testimony enough to the electorate's disenchantment.

Finally, the SDP burst upon the scene. Many who for years have voted for parties which they did not believe represented their political views or who abstained from voting,

1

will now feel able to vote with enthusiasm again. The SDP and its Liberal allies have a great responsibility. For if the Alliance does not work, what democratic alternatives are left?

I should like to take this opportunity to thank all those who contributed their time and special knowledge in helping me to write this book. The views expressed are only mine.

My special thanks go to Mrs Shirley Williams MP who, in an extraordinarily hectic existence, was able to spare me an unhurried hour, and my thanks, in alphabetic order, to Mr Peter Archer QC MP, Mr Mike Blick, Sir Francis Boyd, Lord Brockway, Mr Frank Chapple, Mr Jim Daly to whom I am especially grateful for the material he made available to me and for his valuable comments in the course of a number of conversations, Lord Diamond, Dr Stephen Haseler, Mr John Horam MP, Mr Clive Lindley, Mr Andrew McIntosh, Mr Robert Maclennan MP, Miss Sue Masterman, Mr Brian Murphy who gave me access to his extensive library of Labour Party literature, Dr Henry Pelling, Mr Frank Pickstock, Mr Michael Shanks, Mr Barrie Sherman, Mr Dick Taverne QC and Mr Julian Tobin.

I should also like to thank my publisher John Martin for all his support, Carey Oppenheim for help in ferreting out relevant material from the libraries and Rachel Watson.

London, January 1982

PART I

PROFILE OF THE SDP AT BIRTH: THE FIRST WEEKS

Chapter One

SOCIAL DEMOCRATIC PARTY - ANTIDOTE TO FRUSTRATION

Roy Jenkins returned to London on 6 January 1981, after four years in Brussels away from British politics. It was known that he was disillusioned with the Labour Party he had left behind and that he was ready for a new role in British politics. The question remained: what role should this be? Political circles awaited him with a feeling of expectancy. Would he join the Liberals? Would he launch a new party to transform the face of British politics - something he had talked about during his time in Europe as being both possible and desirable.

Much would depend on who would be willing to leave the Labour Party with him. Initially, this revolved round the so-called Gang of Three, Shirley Williams, David Owen and Bill Rodgers. All former ministers, they were by far the most important dissidents within the Party. The fusion of these two elements - the dissident from Brussels and the three in London - might provide the impetus for a new initiative in British politics and one which some saw as long overdue.

Such a fusion is precisely what occurred. The speed with which it was achieved was astonishing. Within three weeks of Jenkins's return, the four had come together to create a Council for Social Democracy. In another two months, on 26 March 1981, they launched a new party: the Social Democratic Party, the SDP as it became known.

This speed was all the more surprising since not only was the expectant public unaware of the form any new political initiative might take but, on 6 January 1981, the participants themselves had made no joint resolution. All four had been moving at different speeds toward their final decision. Jenkins's return coincided with events within the Labour Party which were forcing others to reconsider their political positions.

Immediately after the special Labour Party conference

Vembley on 24 January, the Gang, now of Four, met at the
Thamesside home of David Owen. That Sunday, 25 January,
they issued their Limehouse Declaration which brought the
Council for Social Democracy into existence. At this stage it
was not intended to convert it into a party until mid-year, or
May at the earliest, but pressures from the public, the media
and the Labour Party itself brought the birth forward. Within
two months the SDP was a reality.

The launch of a new political party in Britain is rare. The
last major political party to emerge successfully was the
Labour Party, created eighty-one years before it spawned the
SDP. Unsuccessful attempts to launch new parties include
Oswald Mosley's New Party of fifty years ago.

Why should the new Social Democratic Party fare any
better? Why should Jenkins, Williams, Owen and Rodgers
believe that they had even a remote chance of success? Given
the electoral system of winner-takes-all in individual
constituencies, a new party or even a small third party, as the
Liberals know to their cost, finds it difficult to win any
parliamentary seats at all.

On the Continent, the emergence of new political parties
is a common event. In Denmark and Norway, for example,
anti-tax parties had an immediate success. In Holland,
Democrats '66 has evolved, doubling its parliamentary
representation in the year of the SDP's creation, 1981. But in
Great Britain the stumbling block has been the British
electoral system and the support which the first-past-the-post
system gives to established parties.

Nothing has demonstrated this more clearly than the
fortunes of the Liberals. In February 1974 they won over 19%
of the vote but only 2% of the seats in the House of Commons:
a paltry fourteen. In a three-party contest, for seats to come
tumbling in, around 30% of the vote has to be won. Coming
second in a host of constituencies, whether in Labour
strongholds in the North or safe Conservative seats in the
rural South, may bring relative glory but it gives no
representation, no influence and no power.

So was it courage or faith, foolhardiness or the gambler's
instinct which launched the Social Democratic Party? To
answer this question involves tracing the story of the SDP's
emergence, its origins in the Labour Party, the pressures
within the party which led towards a rift and the
circumstances which finally made the moment ripe for the
break.

6

One thing is clear. 1981 was the right year for a break-out. It was as if all that had happened in the preceding years was but a preparation, building up toward the *denouement* of 1981 and the creation of the new party. Events seemed to conspire not only to give birth to the party but to give it the greatest chance of healthy life. If it does not survive and flourish, it could not have wished for better growing conditions.

Over the years there has been talk of a re-alignment of British politics. Since the war a philosophical, emotional and finally political rift had existed inside the Labour party. While the Left had no electorally convincing place to go, the Right always had the option of moving into the centre to combine with the Liberal Party, and the Liberal Party's parliamentary impotence meant that it was usually available for discussion and serious consideration of re-alignment.

As the Left grew stronger throughout the seventies, it did so at its peril, for it created pressure on the Right to leave the Party altogether. But other conditions had to be favourable for the Right to take the plunge. Had the scenario been custom-written for such an event, conditions in 1981 could hardly have been more ideal.

British politics had polarised. Not only had the Labour Party lurched to the Left, but the Conservative Party had moved significantly to the Right. With the former prime minister, Edward Heath replaced by Margaret Thatcher, the Tory Party had radically changed in style and character. To the surprise of observers, the old pragmatic party which knew how to adapt to changing circumstances became a hard-line, inflexible movement. The Conservative Party, in its dismay at losing the 1974 election, had opted for a woman and a relatively junior but tough politician to whom the Russians subsequently referred as the Iron Lady, a name which was to persist.

In due course, following a long series of strikes during the winter of 1978/79, the Conservatives won the May 1979 general election. For those wishing to vote other than Labour there was only one hard-line ideology on offer.

The incoming government now pursued a monetarist economic policy which it claimed was the only way of bringing down inflation. Though many people were impressed by a politician who seemed to be a leader figure, styling herself a conviction politician and intent on a consistent policy, disillusion soon set in. Whatever the merits of a tight

7

monetary policy in the long term, the immediate results were mainly bad. Unemployment rose relentlessly to record levels of three million, with school-leavers particularly affected. Inflation rose steeply. Dear money brought a rash of bankruptcies. Restricted budgets hit schools and hospitals. Unprecedented riots erupted in London and many provincial cities, presumed to stem in part from unemployment and adverse social conditions.

In such a situation the popularity of the Conservative government was not enhanced by Mrs Thatcher's unwillingness to adapt to the exceptional circumstances. While many of her ministers individually indicated their unease, the government did not change course.

Against this background, of the new-style doctrinaire Conservative government, and a Labour Party further left than ever before and tearing itself apart, the SDP surfaced. The political seas had parted as if by magic, leaving the centre ground of British politics free for the first time in recent history.

Opinion polls had been indicating that, should a new alignment of the centre be realised, more people would vote for it than for either Labour or Conservative Parties. Arguably these findings were an indication of disaffection with the major parties, not necessarily evidence of support for a centre party; however, they indicated the foundation upon which any future party might build.

The route to that point of disaffection is a long one to trace, but is revealing of the nature of the SDP and its support. The Limehouse Declaration refers to "the sterile and rigid framework into which the British political system has increasingly fallen in the last two decades". It is as if, over those twenty years, the electorate had increasingly tried to manoeuvre itself out of the rigid framework, to escape the straitjacket of the two-party system. For the two-party system had been found wanting; the recurrent signals of discontent rose ever more distinctly as the electorate attempted to find an alternative to the solutions on offer. But while it tested the fabric of the straightjacket, causing it to bulge in various places, it found no adequate release mechanism. The Social Democratic Party offered that release.

Frustration has been a thread running unbroken through British society for these past twenty years: a realisation for most of that time that, while things were improving, they were improving too slowly, that others in neighbouring continental countries were doing better and overtaking our standard of living. The feeling was that our "once great country", which had dominated the map of the world, had lost its way.

The electorate has tended to put the blame for political and economic failure on numerous groups and social tendencies: the trade unions, coloured immigrants, the permissive society, so-called national characteristics of indolence, the media, social divisions and so on. But in the last analysis it has held politicians and political parties responsible.

Disillusion over the years found expression in desertion from the major parties. Increasingly, people turned to the Liberals, the Scottish Nationalists, the Welsh Nationalists, or the National Front, or preferred to lend support to pressure groups - from the Campaign for Nuclear Disarmament to Shelter, from Concern for the Aged to Oxfam. At general elections, fewer people voted for the major parties. At by-elections the swings against the party of government became more violent. Fewer and fewer people bothered to vote at all. Many felt disenfranchised and preferred to abstain.

The growing disillusion of the nation found an echo within the political party system itself. Tensions increased, both inside the Labour Party and in confrontation between the parties. This political infighting in turn exacerbated the dismay of the electorate.

The dissatisfaction of the British electorate will be discussed at length in Chapter Thirteen. For the moment all that need be said is that the soil was fertile for the Social Democrats. If the Gang of Four took their time before making the final decision to launch the party, it was because it was still a voyage into the unknown. Only the first stage was clearly charted. The risks to personal careers were considerable, nor could allegiance to the Labour Party be abandoned lightly.

This uncertainty, even danger, was expressed by Peter Jenkins, writing in the *Guardian* about a possible re-alignment of the Centre Left, months before it had happened: "It could take a long while, perhaps extend over two or three elections; meanwhile, promising careers will be wasted in the wilderness. ... Those who set out had better be prepared for a long haul into the unknown."

The Gang of Four finally decided that conditions were auspicious enough to hazard their careers. They launched the Social Democratic Party on 26 March 1981 and waited. They did not have long to wait.

9

Chapter Two

SDP: FIRST SUCCESSES

Within ten days the Social Democratic Party numbered 43,588 members. The response was extraordinary. It was as if the frustration of years had been unblocked by the announcement of a new political party. Those who had regarded themselves as disenfranchised could now not only vote again but become involved in their community. These feelings were particularly strong among Labour Party supporters who felt that their party had changed over the years and who now had a spiritual home to move to. How often the cry was heard that "this is not the Party I joined. I am not leaving the Labour Party, it's the Party that has left me."

However, it was not only Labour people who were joining the Social Democrats. Conservatives who would not have considered defecting to a left-wing Labour party now saw in the SDP a possible alternative. Conservatism did not seem to be working, and the loyalties of Conservative voters were under considerable strain. Tough single-minded Thatcher speeches might find favour with the hard core or with devotees of the new monetarist ideology but the mass of rank and file Conservatives greeted them with varying degrees of unease. Some began to move to the Social Democrats. Those who had voted Liberal for want of an acceptable Labour party now felt that their original party had come back to them, that some form of Labour Party was again available - a party of conscience and reform. Many who had opted out of active politics altogether, had never wished to join a party, or had stopped voting, now felt motivated to join the SDP and even become active in it.

Political meetings became a rival attraction to television and the public house as the SDP pulled in full houses. Three hundred people at a meeting was not unusual. Double that figure not unknown. Men and women at first came somewhat shyly, uncertain of what acquaintances from other areas of their lives they might meet, or perhaps uneasy at the prospect of meeting former Labour colleagues.

The movement gathered momentum, propelled by the energy of the leaders. The Gang of Four addressed two hundred meetings in the space of two months, each averaging one meeting a day, covering all parts of the country. The atmosphere at these meetings was all 'go'. Political controversy had vanished. Harmony was in the air. People felt united in a common endeavour. Many who had previously been used to attending Labour discussion meetings were particularly refreshed by the friendliness of the atmosphere: the absence of the bitterness and animosity which had increasingly corroded local and national meetings was as striking as stillness after continuous noise. In modern idiom, the vibes were good.

All over the country, groups were forming, holding their first meeting, and taking the first steps toward setting up a local Social Democratic group. Everything was new. Everything had to be created from scratch. Some help was available from the Party headquarters in Queen Anne's Gate, and a national party constitution was evolving, but each local group worked on its own with the enthusiasm of pioneers, fired by a sense of urgency and mission.

It would be no exaggeration to say that many saw the SDP as a belated if not final chance to do something positive to arrest a national decline which had been continuous over the years and had been accelerating noticeably of late. It was a chance to work with like-minded people and, instead of opposing people in one's own party, to put forward ideas and to have them listened to. These ideas might not be accepted by the group, but nor would they be received with the hisses and boos which had so often distinguished the Labour Left's reaction to the Right in Labour Party forums of the 1970s. Anger could once again be directed outwards, against the wrongs afflicting society. Political action could again become constructive and outward-looking rather than sectarian, destructive and inward-looking.

All over the country a wide range of the British public was joining. Early membership was divided one fifth from London, four fifths from the rest of the country. The SDP could boast that members came from every constituency in the country including those of Michael Foot and Margaret Thatcher. Academics, journalists, civil servants, scientists, teachers, doctors, lawyers, all were joining in great numbers. A league of Social Democratic lawyers was founded. Manual

11

workers and trade unionists also joined, and indeed a shop steward and shipyard fitter won a council seat in Durham for the SDP on the day of the Warrington by-election. However, as critics were quick to point out, SDP membership was mainly middle-class. Supporters countered with the assertion that this is normal, that social reform movements are started by the intelligentsia. Certainly support was particularly marked in the university towns.

The label of middle-class was accentuated in other ways. Membership was not cheap. At £9, it entailed more of a financial consideration than joining the other parties. Furthermore, it could be paid by credit card or cheque.

However, the SDP was not shy of being modern. Its aim was to stimulate membership fast and to collect information. Still, dependence on modern technology can create its own headaches: the Midland Bank computer, which the Party was using to record all new subscriptions, was affected by a bank clerks' dispute and all the data was locked inside it. Embarrassing weeks elapsed before computer print-outs became available. During that time the SDP leadership had no way of ascertaining the geographical disposition of its membership, nor could contact be fostered between those who had joined.

As people thronged to pay their £9, the first wave of parliamentarians, in both the House of Commons and the Lords, made their new allegiance known. Eleven Labour MPs and one Tory joined David Owen and Bill Rodgers in a relatively modest Parliamentary Party, fourteen members strong but already outstripping the Liberals' eleven. It was not yet great representation, but it was a promising foundation on which to build.

The solitary Tory was Christopher Brocklebank-Fowler, a former chairman of the Conservative Bow Group. The eleven Labour MPs who crossed over first included a number of former Parliamentary Private Secretaries, nearly all of whom had worked under ministers who were to become SDP leaders: Ian Wrigglesworth had been PPS to Home Secretary Roy Jenkins in 1974-76 and Tom Bradley had likewise been PPS to Jenkins, as well as chairman of Labour's National Executive Committee. John Horam, Edward Lyons, Tom Ellis and John Roper had all worked under Rodgers at different times. Robert Maclennan and John Cartwright had worked under Shirley Williams: Maclennan on Prices and Consumer Protection, and Cartwright at the Ministry of Education and Science.

Cartwright had also twice been a member of the NEC. Richard Crawshaw was Deputy Speaker. In 1972 he had also established a world non-stop walking record of 225.8 miles, promising much-needed stamina.

This was the first wave of defections. The hope was that as it became more obvious that the SDP was not a nine days' wonder but was here to stay, the movement would snowball and other MPs, mainly from Labour, would cross the floor. The first additional convert came in July: Jim Wellbeloved; more were to come during the first SDP conference in October.

In the initial impulse a rather larger number of Lords than MPs declared themselves for Social Democracy. Clearly, it was a less drastic step for them since their future careers were not subject to periodic re-election. Among them were former ministers: Lord Aylestone, who as Herbert Bowden had been cabinet minister and subsequently chairman of the Independent Broadcasting Authority; Lord Diamond, former cabinet minister and Chairman of the Royal Commission on Distribution of Income and Wealth; the Lords Harris, Donaldson, Walston, Winterbottom and Kennet. Other notables included Lord Hunt, leader of the first successful expedition to conquer Mount Everest, Lord Young, President of the Consumers' Association, Lord Bullock, Lord Perry, former Vice Chancellor of the Open University, and the publisher Lord Weidenfeld.

Ultimately all parties depend not just on leaders and activists but on the ranks of ordinary sympathisers and voters. No-one could confidently predict how many would put their crosses next to SDP candidates until a by-election took place. By-elections had been very few since the general election in May 1979, the last having been fought a year before.

Till the Warrington by-election was fought in July, opinion polls taken by the major political research companies such as Gallup, National Opinion Polls (NOP) and Market and Opinion Research International (MORI) had to provide the main evidence of voting intentions.

From the very frequent studies carried out by these organisations and published in the national newspapers, two things soon became evident.

First, the Social Democratic party had support. Second, in partnership with the Liberals, this became significant. Support for a hypothetical alliance between the two parties was seen to be greater than the sum of support commanded by the parties individually. While neither Liberals nor SDP seemed strong enough to win individual constituencies, and certainly not elections, the allied cause produced figures so extraordinarily high that they drew reservations from the Social Democrats themselves and scepticism from the opposition parties. Gallup polls published in the *Daily Telegraph* asked: "If the new Social Democratic party made an alliance with the Liberals so that a candidate from only one of these parties would stand in each constituency, how would you vote?" The response, over a period which went back to 19 March 1981, before the SDP had been launched, was remarkably consistent.

	19 Mar	*2 Apr*	*16 Apr*	*14 May*
	%	%	%	%
SDP/Liberal	46	48.5	45	40
Labour	27	24.5	28	28.5
Conservative	25	25.5	25.5	28.5
Others	2	1.5	1.5	3

To be successful the SDP and the Liberal Party clearly had to work together. United they were leading. Separately as third and fourth parties, they remained small. Jenkins had always planned to work with the Liberals, either by personally joining their ranks or, in the event, through an alliance between the two parties.

There was little separating them. Their political visions were remarkably similar. They agreed about the main domestic issues such as the mixed economy and foreign policies of Common Market and NATO - an international role for Britain. The SDP leaders enjoyed good relations with the Liberal leader, David Steel. A partnership between the parties seemed as natural as it was advantageous.

From the earliest days of the new party discussions took place and a practical alliance was created. Though the alliance was not formally approved by the Liberal membership till their annual conference in Llandudno in September, it got off to an excellent start, crucial for the SDP's future development. The informal alliance's greatest success at this initial stage came with the Warrington by-election, for this showed that the two parties could co-operate to the benefit of both, the Liberals standing down in favour of Roy Jenkins and then giving selfless support in the campaign. The excellent Warrington result (the subject of a later chapter) confirmed Gallup's figures in a situation where the Alliance fields one candidate only.

The forging of a working alliance was one of the most important early successes for the SDP, making it a serious contender for power.

Chapter Three

SDP: WHY NO POLICIES?

The criticism most often heard about the early SDP was that the party had no policies. Not only those hostile but sympathisers and even SDP members would make the same point. Where were the detailed policies on housing, education, taxation, industrial democracy, reform of the House of Lords, London Transport fares structures, to name but a few?

If the small print of policies did not exist in the first weeks of the party's existence, the leadership had ready explanations, referring to the Manifestoitis which plagued the other parties. They were suggesting that this practice could lead to inflexible policies developed too early.

More important was that for a party claiming to be founded on the concept of the widest democracy, policy-making had to involve the membership. Policy could not be imposed but had to be evolved in co-operation with the constituencies. This process would clearly take time, since a constitution had to be agreed, formalising the relationship between headquarters and the party in the country. The constituency parties also needed first to organise themselves locally and make their contribution to creating policies.

Nevertheless, the SDP did have policies, even if these were only sketched in broad outline. They were clear from the outset - made public in the original Limehouse Declaration and the party's "Twelve tasks for Social Democrats". They fell into three categories.

The first concerned the structure of politics; the second the country's home policies: how to make the economy grow, and how to achieve a more equitable society; and the third dealt with international relations. These three categories of policy were interdependent - incorporating a unified vision.

To examine each in turn, how did the Social Democrats wish to change the structure of British politics? Through electoral reform and through decentralisation and a greater attention to the workings of democracy at all levels in society.

In this way it was intended to build a society which functioned on the principles of consensus rather than opposition and involvement rather than apathy. Policies would not be subject to constant change, as in the past, and would have the necessary democratic support to make them effective.

Taking electoral reform first. In the existing system, where one million votes have elected two or three Liberal MPs as against twenty-five Tory or Labour MPs, there seemed a miscarriage of elementary democratic justice. In the British first-past-the-post system, where losers' votes are worthless, election results lead to misrepresentation of the electorate's wishes. Governments can be elected in some cases on a minority vote - the Conservatives in 1951 and Labour in 1929 and 1974 are examples. Proportional representation was the key.

Equally important, the bias of politics would change. For example, with proportional representation, the three elections since February 1974 would all have brought in coalition governments, since no party would have been the outright winner. While Labour and Conservatives are favoured by the present system, and claim this makes for strong government, the SDP says otherwise: apart from evidence of recent governments' lack of success, the SDP maintains that the system has encouraged adversary politics, causing each new government to make radical changes to the outgoing government's policies. This lack of continuity is seen as one of the main reasons for the country's continuing economic decline.

Proportional representation was more likely to bring about consensus and co-operation within each coalition government, and less change after a change of government. Continuity would enable the country to plan more effectively, for industry to make steady progress, for governments to end zigzag policy-making.

The SDP sought to stimulate people's energy and commitment not only through a fairer system in the polling booths but through decentralisation and more decision-making down the line. They advocated the 'small is beautiful' philosophy of a society broken up into smaller, more accessible units, whether in local administration, in schools or in hospitals. This was intended to bring more power to the regions and the nations of Britain: it was argued that the men in Whitehall, whether Ministers or civil servants, do not always know best. Every citizen should be able to find out about and challenge executive decisions. This greater democracy would lead to better policies at home and abroad.

As to the more conventional policies, these were stated clearly.

Economic policy would have the mixed economy as its cornerstone, "without constant Conservative sniping at the public sector or repeated Labour threats to private enterprise." An upturn in Britain's economic fortunes required "a consistent economic strategy ... not disrupted every few years by a political upheaval." The nation's temporary oil wealth should be invested in new industries, new jobs and regional rehabilitation. Money should be pumped into vital manufacturing industry, into communications, into public transport and the improvement of the environment. A flexible incomes policy was to be developed to strike a balance between more employment and unacceptable inflation.

In its response to the questions of employment the SDP aimed to be truthful rather than optimistic. False promises would not create full employment in a world of recession and of new labour-saving technologies. Investment, coupled with specific measures such as apprenticeships and youth training programmes and the like, would help, but the SDP believed would help achieve fuller, not full employment. This problem had been growing over the past decade and could not just be made to disappear.

Likewise, in the area of social progress, the SDP laid down broad guidelines rather than specific measures. This approach inevitably drew the fire of critics, who suggested that pious hopes were no substitute for detailed and tested measures. What, for example, was meant by: "We are pledged to improve the quality of our health services, our housing and the education of our children, and to make these and other community services more responsive to people's needs, not least in the inner cities"?

A more precise statement seemed particularly necessary on the subject of education. Did improving the quality of schools include abolishing the private sector, or did it really just mean making comprehensive schools better? It had soon become clear that while Shirley Williams, former Minister for Education, wished to do away with fee-paying schools, her colleagues did not agree.

As for foreign policies, the Social Democratic outlook was unambiguously international and the party's statements were more specific than in most other areas. A number of the

18

planks supporting this international attitude were well-documented points of divergence within the Labour Party, past and present. The SDP stated that "Britain should co-operate in the world and not retreat into sour isolation. We need our friends in a dangerous world, which means playing our full part in the European community and in NATO, vigorously pursuing multilateral but not unilateral disarmament."

This was in contradistinction to Labour policy which, as in the past, was coming down against Britain's participation in the EEC and opting for unilateral disarmament.

The Social Democratic Party supported the Brandt commission. It accepted the need to give active support to the Third World, for "without imaginative generosity, which marches alongside far-sighted self-interest, we shall not only frustrate the hopes of the developing world, but undermine our own long-term prosperity".

The Social Democrats saw themselves as a progressive party of the left centre, and considered this more important than a full portfolio of detailed policies. The hallmark of the party was consensus to carry out radical policies democratically. It was the spirit of the party, of tolerance and reform, which the SDP judged would be the overriding factor in taking people along with it.

Chapter Four

THE LEADERSHIP

If the fledgling Social Democratic Party was criticised for being short on policies, it could not be criticised for being short on leaders. This quadrumvirate had not been planned but, having emerged, it had certain advantages, at least in the initial stages.

Novelty value not least of all. It meant greater media interest and more editorial coverage. To have the equivalent of four Margaret Thatchers or four Michael Foots addressing meetings all over the country and being available for television, radio and newspaper interviews was a boon, multiplying the party leadership's normal exposure to the public.

It was also added incentive for local political groups organising a meeting to know that whoever of the Gang of Four gave a speech was a leader. They were not being fobbed off with number two, three or four. Audiences likewise were more appreciative and responsive and probably bigger.

For a party priding itself on a special democratic impetus, the collective leadership intensified the aura of democracy. All voices were equal inside the leadership group. Yet it was clear that the group mechanism was not universally liked nor accepted as final. The question kept coming up: "When will you have one leader? Who is the leader to be?" David Steel, leader of the Liberals, expressed the view that communications within the Alliance would be easier if leader could meet leader. One SDP MP stated: "Most of our members believe that permanent arrangements must provide for a more conventional structure at the top."

Yet there are precedents for the less than conventional. The Labour Party itself did not have a formal leader till 1922. Before then, it made do with 'Chairman of the Parliamentary Party'. In post-Tito Yugoslavia there is a presidential council of eight members, each in turn acting as president. Dual leadership exists in various countries, even if without formal provision in a constitution. In the Soviet Union, Kruschev and Bulganin, later Brezhnev and Kosygin, represented the country jointly, till one from each pair emerged as the clear leader. In the United States, Nixon, though President, was aided by a charismatic, peripatetic foreign minister, and for many in the United States and outside, Nixon and Kissinger seemed to be running the affairs of the country jointly.

There are also precedents of shared leadership in Western Europe. In those early days the Social Democrats often alluded to their namesakes, the Social Democratic Party of West Germany (Sozialdemokratische Partei Deutschlands). Not only was this close to home, but the German party's formula could be relevant. A feeling was emerging that, as Helmut Schmidt was parliamentary leader and Willy Brandt was head of the party, a similar division in leadership functions could help the SDP.

Roy Jenkins and Shirley Williams had both emerged as favourites for leader. A dual leadership, it was felt, could capitalise on their complementary strengths to the advantage of the party. Jenkins had the international reputation, while Williams was the best-known and best-liked in Great Britain.

All four deserved to be considered though. All were leaders individually in their own right. All had been senior ministers and were people of political weight. Nevertheless, Roy Jenkins and Shirley Williams did emerge as the two people who in their different ways were seen as the future leaders of the Social Democratic movement. This view, generally held by the membership in the country and by the Parliamentary Party, directly influenced the drafting of the Party Constitution. The proposition to go forward for democratic approval by the SDP in 1982 would include a twin leadership for parliament and party at large.

Jenkins at 61 was the elder statesman. He had a distinguished reputation at home and abroad, having just spent four years as President of the European Commission. Before that he had been an excellent Chancellor of the Exchequer and Home Secretary in the Harold Wilson government of the late sixties, becoming deputy leader of the Labour Party.

In 1970 Jenkins had been seen as a future leader of his party. However, the dispute over British entry into the Common Market led him to resign his position of deputy leader, and left him increasingly isolated within the Labour Party. Disappointingly for him, he was given the job of Home

Secretary a second time from 1974 to 1976, drew his conclusions, resigned from the House of Commons and accepted the important post offered in Brussels.

However, the Common Market dispute within Labour had given Jenkins another role as unofficial leader of the right-wing Jenkinsites, a group of seventy or so MPs. That mantle, a little dusty by the time Jenkins returned from Brussels, nevertheless could still be donned. However, reactions to this were mixed. Jenkins had something of the man of yesterday about him, having been out of British politics for four years. Some saw him now as too liberal, too much in the centre, others as lacking political toughness and electoral appeal. His supporters could point to his record in office, to his intellectual achievements, from a first-class degree in Politics, Philosophy and Economics at Balliol, Oxford, to elegantly written biographies of Asquith and Attlee.

In any event, Roy Jenkins was the man whose vision had made the Social Democratic Party possible. Round his ideas, expressed while he was still EEC president, people prepared for the new political party. When he returned, his contribution was the necessary spur to action. Any doubts about his suitability as leader were dispelled during his Warrington by-election campaign. Jenkins was accepted as a political fighter. The only remaining problem was to return to the House of Commons through another by-election at the earliest opportunity.

Shirley Williams also needed to get back into Parliament, since she had lost her seat in the 1979 elections. She was to return first to the House after a dramatic contest in Crosby.

Mrs Williams had also achieved highest office in Wilson and Callaghan governments, first as Minister for Prices and Consumer Protection, later as Minister for Education and Science. For eleven years (1970 to 1981) she had been a member of the National Executive Committee of the Labour Party. More than that, Shirley Williams has a charismatic personality. People like her and trust her. She is that rare politician in any party who seems to be without side, who speaks from the heart and not like a professional politician. In many ways she was the perfect contrast to the Conservative leader, Margaret Thatcher. Shirley Williams was clearly the party's greatest electoral asset.

The view soon evolved that Mrs Williams would be the best person to lead the party to victory as party president, while Jenkins would lead the Parliamentary SDP and, in the event of victory, would run the affairs of state as prime minister.

Had competition for leader been less fierce, David Owen might well have been a front runner. Owen had had a remarkable career, and since the middle of 1980 had been the most committed to the cause of Social Democracy. He saw the SDP as an alternative progressive party with a cutting edge, stressing that he was not interested in 'just soft, soggy centrism'. Of the four, he was the most intent on retaining an identity quite separate from the Liberals. Hence his relations with them sometimes also had a cutting edge.

David Owen was a research doctor at St Thomas's Hospital in London up to the time he was elected Member of Parliament for Plymouth Sutton. He won the seat from the Conservatives. He was the first medical man this century to win one of the high offices of state. In February 1977, when Anthony Crosland died, Owen was appointed Foreign Secretary as his successor. At 38, he was the youngest man in the job since Anthony Eden.

The fourth member of the Gang, Bill Rodgers, was the least well known. Only with the advent of the SDP has his name become a household name. Minister of Transport in the last Labour Government, Rodgers has a long history on the moderate wing of the Labour movement. From 1953 to 1960 he was secretary of the Fabian Society. He then took over the running of the Campaign for Democratic Socialism to back Gaitskell against the unilateralists, where he also made his name as a man with organisational skill. Rodgers has been in Parliament since 1962. Although he is an impressive public speaker, organiser and leader, given the competition of Jenkins and Williams, he could not be considered a realistic choice.

The SDP election of one or, more likely, two leaders would probably not be settled till 1982, after a constitutional conference. A method of election would then be adopted, involving either the total membership of the Parliamentary SDP, or a combination of the two. Although many of the membership would favour Mrs Williams, Jenkins looked the winner for job of parliamentary leader whichever method was selected.

Looking further ahead, some might speculate about the next generation of leaders. People closest to the centre were beginning to speak of David Owen, and of David Steel, looking forward to the future Alliance with the Liberals. Both men were in their early forties. Would one be the natural successor to Roy Jenkins?

PART II

THE OLD LABOUR PARTY: SOCIAL DEMOCRATIC HERITAGE

Chapter Five

WHAT IS LABOUR? THE SENTIMENTAL MYTH

To understand the SDP, one must look at its parent, Labour. But the concept of Labour is as elusive as the concept of happiness, as intangible as the essence of England, or of the Irish, or of sex appeal. Any attempt to answer the question "What is Labour?" founders in a complex reality. Immediate, instinctive responses to the question would be diverse, aroused by the complexities of history, of heroes and anti-heroes, sentiment and prejudice, policies and philosophies, faith and intolerance. And the SDP inherits some of the complexities of its parent.

The Labour movement is united largely by force of sentiment and tradition. In the Conservative Party, sentiment is on the whole turned outward - toward Queen and country, and in the old days toward Empire. In the Labour Party sentiment is turned inward - on the Party itself. The love which the party inspires can turn to hatred, and expressions of animosity, which within Tory ranks are generally reserved for enemies without, are in the Labour Party often directed at enemies within.

In 1981, at a time when the Conservatives had achieved exceptional unpopularity - even by the standards of mid-term governments - Labour was fighting internally. With unemployment figures breaking all records, the Labour Party had little energy left to fight the Conservatives, so busy was it with internal wars between its Left and Right, Left and Left, and Right and Right.

The main struggle between the wings of the Party was on the issue of party democracy; the resolution of this issue also determines who runs the Party. The questions of European policy, unilateral nuclear disarmament, and the abolition of the House of Lords became subsidiary, important though they were.

The fighting within each Labour wing is tactical, each faction concerned with the promotion of its own proposition.

27

For the Right, it ultimately became a question of whether to fight inside the Party or outside it. For the Left, the issue was whether to go on attacking until it gained total control, or whether to call a halt and to settle for the power already gained - a major concern being the risk of pushing ever more moderates into the embrace of the Social Democrats now waiting outside its ranks.

The fight is for power, but it is for power in the Party and through the Party. And in the fight over the Party, reality merges with sentiment. Both sides have grown up in the Party. Both see it as their Party. Its tradition, its ritual, its rhetoric are part of them - as is its crusade. It is the Party they love and claim as their own. When two parents quarrel, which one loves the children more? Do Beethoven and Goethe 'belong' to East Germany or West Germany? Labour is a deeply sentimental party. It is this sentiment which has united the Party. This emotion is frequently expressed. Gaitskell promised to "fight and fight and fight again to save the party we love". Roy Hattersley, in an interview with the late Robert Mackenzie, said: "I will never join another political party. I was born in the Labour Party and I'll die in the Labour Party." Labour MP Austin Mitchell, speaking about his colleague, John Sever, the first MP not to be re-selected under the new procedure, claimed that "he had worked hard and loyally for the party he still loves." Does one love a party? Or think one does? Or is this part of the obligatory ritual attached to Labour Party membership? Like the ritual of joining hands at Conference and singing 'Auld Lang Syne'?

Clearly there is an overlap between sentiment and reality. There is the reality of the Welfare State which looks after people from the cradle to the grave, one of the great compassionate achievements of the twentieth century, and there is the myth of a party blessed by God, or at any rate one which makes ample reference to religious connections: the Broad Church party which is, in Harold Wilson's words, "more than a political organisation: it is a crusade, or it would be better that it did not exist."

There are the many real achievements that Labour can point to, from the creation of the National Health Service to the establishment of the Open University; from the dismantling of the old Empire to the outlawing of sex and race discrimination in jobs and housing. Those are the historical realities which unite those in the Party whether of Left or Right - solid achievements to view with pride and attachment.

Left and Right use the same political jargon to express sentiment and to further myth, though here the Left makes the running. It is their vocabulary which carries the day. Who can be less than fervent if the goal at the end of the road is utopia? Being a moderate sounds wishy-washy. Being a Socialist sounds principled, concrete and full of conviction. So being a Socialist is what is important. For some this is the kernel. For others it is the necessary show. For the majority it is the sentimental essence of a unifying phraseology.

In the ethos which has grown up over the years, Socialism is a kind of virility symbol. It is what separates the men from the boys, the fighter from the dilettante, and gives moral vindication. It is a credential that an emigre from the Labour Party leaves behind.

Hence the need for the new party to retain its link with the word "Socialist", or at very least "Social". Good loyal members of the clan need to indicate that they are continuing the fight in the old, morally-approved tradition. They may be outside the old framework, but they have not changed. Rather it is their former party which has changed. Like the Free French under de Gaulle, they are the true standard bearers, while the leadership left behind on the mainland is unrepresentative of the established cause.

That is why Socialist is such an emotive word. For David Owen to insist he is a Socialist is a sentimental attitude rather than a claim with a precise meaning. Socialist means too many different things for different people for it to be otherwise. Fenner Brockway, an old-fashioned utopian Socialist, takes another view: "Yes, David Owen says he is a Socialist, that he learnt all he knows about Socialism from me. I only wish to God I had taught him better."

Those who do not choose to employ the hallowed vocabulary are prime targets for enemies within Labour. Roy Jenkins for example attracts the jibe that "Roy has not used the word Socialist for years", as if such lip-service were the criterion for effective, progressive politics. Similarly, during the Warrington by-election Harold Wilson was dismissive in the best Wilsonian way: "Roy? More of a socialite than Socialist".

Bryan Magee (Labour MP for Leyton until he left the Party in January 1982) evokes George Orwell's *1984* in his piece on 'Socialist Newspeak' (*Observer*, 22 February 1981). He recalls two separate conversations with two successful Labour politicians at a time when he was new to Labour politics. Their advice, quite independent of each other, went like this: 'If they ask you what housing policy we ought to have, tell them what we need is a Socialist housing policy - in ringing tones and with lots of passion. If it's education, say we need a Socialist education policy. And so on. Nobody knows what it means, and it doesn't commit you to anything, but they love it, and they'll support you to the hilt. '

Magee also pinpoints the disparity between Labour politicians' pragmatic way of proceeding, whether in Westminster or in the country, and the rhetoric they employ, couched in "'isms' and religious metaphors". Labour politicians, he says, are "effortlessly bilingual". Few actually believe in full-blooded Socialism, yet "we all pay lip-service to Socialism ... because we are supposed to be Socialists we shut up about not being."

Yet what is full-blooded Socialism? If one looks to Crosland's *The Future of Socialism* for guidance, he confirms that the word has no definitive meaning: "it has none and never could". He points to the many different historical meanings of socialism which define it variously in terms of ownership, co-operation, planning, and income distribution. Karl Marx's definition, however, is the one which was adopted in 1918 by the Labour Party as part of the new constitution drafted by Sydney Webb. This was the famous Clause 4, unsuccessfully challenged by Gaitskell in 1959, which exists to this day. It is, as every member of the Labour Party will confirm, still there printed in his membership card. It is the Clause referring to nationalisation, or, in its full form: "To secure for the workers by hand or by brain the full fruits of their industry and the most equitable distribution thereof that may be possible upon the basis of common ownership of the means of production, distribution, and exchange, and the best obtainable system of popular administration and control of each industry or service."

This definition became the litmus paper to test socialism and Gaitskell was unable to change this. Yet, Gaitskell, Crosland, Magee and like-minded Labour politicians have sought to concentrate on the ends of socialism rather than get bogged down on the means, of which nationalisation could be one. For these politicians, the end is the achievement of a certain kind of society, based on certain moral values and aspirations. Crosland pinpoints some of the underlying ideals which, historically, have united socialist thinking and which give the word Socialism meaning: protest against material poverty, concern for social welfare, belief in equality and the classless society, ideals of fraternity and co-operation, and against mass unemployment.

The movement is about the realisation of these ideals. The means may vary from time to time. And yet everyone in the Labour movement must either believe in nationalisation as the fundamental issue of socialism, or pay lip-service to it, or explain it away - as for instance Roy Hattersley does by claiming that "Common Ownership" does not necessarily mean nationalisation.

But public ownership and nationalisation is the *sine qua non* of the movement, the sacred cow of socialism. In the broadest sense of the word, nationalisation has become the 'sentimental' purpose of the movement, and Socialism its sentimental designation. Even Crosland, though redefining the word, opted for *The Future of Socialism* for the title of his book.

Chapter Six

BRITISH SOCIALISM - CONSENSUS STYLE

The British Labour Party was founded as the political arm of the British Trade Union movement. At a time when conditions for working men were already improving, faster progress needed more direct involvement from those concerned. Although the Liberal Party was the party of reform, its interests did not always coincide with those of the under-privileged. The moment had come for labour to have its own representatives in the House of Commons.

The Labour Party, or the Labour Representation Committee (LRC) as it was known in 1900 when it was founded, was the creature of the trade unions, mainly the unions of the unskilled. Then, as now, the trade unions provided nearly all the finance. The three Socialist societies which, together with the unions, constituted the LRC, were soon in disarray. The Social Democratic Federation, marxist (and quite unrelated to the 1980s version of the Social Democrats), opted out within a year, because the LRC was not marxist enough. The Fabians crossed swords with the ILP (Independent Labour Party) because they did not want to transform the LRC into a new political party.

The Labour Representation Committee was initially just what its name indicated. It was not a party. It had not decided whether to establish itself as one, or whether to work with one of the major parties. It had no political programme. It was to become a real party soon enough. Within six years, the number of LRC MPs had swelled to twenty-nine, brought in on the tide of the Liberal triumph in the 1906 election. The Labour Representation Committee became the Labour Party.

The nature of its birth left a permanent mark on the Party. It was a peculiarly British creation, uninfluenced by doctrine, unsure where it was going or how it would get there. It just knew that the working man's interests needed greater attention. The rest would be worked out pragmatically, with the passage of time, in response to events.

British socialism was born with the working man as its founder, his needs as its objective, and his condition as its inspiration. At its core was the labour movement with its strong traditions and loyalties, its class feeling, its reluctance and slowness to change that it shared with the rest of Britain. It was both an engine for change and a braking mechanism.

This peculiar form of socialism became known to many admirers and detractors as Labourism. Labourism was for the here and now. It existed to improve working conditions, to increase the pay packet, above all to ensure a job. It wanted bread today. Doctrines and ideals were for socialist thinkers, and these were thin on the ground in Britain; indeed, according to Engels, it was "the indifference to theory which is one of the chief reasons of the slow progress of the English working-class movement."

Nevertheless, various socialist ideologies did provide an emotional attachment and intellectual background to Labourism. Among the most important were Christian Socialism, Fabianism and Marxism. All three sought in their different ways to do away with the capitalist society.

Christian Socialists believed in a Christian brotherhood of man. They sought to eliminate private property and to replace it with communal ownership. Fabians believed in all manner of collective action, not just aiming at collective ownership. Part of their early motto - "For the right moment you must wait, as Fabius did most patiently warring against Hannibal ..." - emphasised the Fabians' gradualist approach. They believed that every step forward taken within the capitalist system was a step toward Socialism.

Not so the Marxists, who believed that no good at all could come out of the capitalist state. It must first be overthrown. Only then should the state become the collective owner of the means of production.

Marxism did not take root at the beginning of the century in this country, removed as it was from the experiments on the Continent. Although the 1917 Russian Revolution was observed with excitement, this was not seen as charting the way for the British working-class movement. Nevertheless, when Labour's revised constitution was drawn up by Sidney Webb in the following year, it included the famous Clause 4, making common ownership of the means of production the fundamental objective of British socialism.

In the 1930s, the inclination to turn to Marx for an

intellectual understanding and stimulus to action became increasingly evident. To quote Crosland: "Under the impact of the 1931 slump and the growth of Fascism, more and more people came to mistrust a merely *ad hoc* reformist approach, and to feel that some more thorough-going analysis was needed to explain the catastrophe which appeared to be engulfing world capitalism." In other words, they believed that to bring about major socialist reform "capitalism itself must first be forcibly overthrown."

And so to the first post-war Labour Government, the first time Labour had a majority, no longer needing the support of other political parties in order to govern. It was the most memorable government since the Liberal Government of 1906, a government which transformed British society in the most fundamental way by the initiation of the Welfare State, freeing people (up to a point) from the financial burdens of falling ill or growing old, and introducing the idea of care 'from the cradle to the grave'.

A major programme of nationalisation, for which the way had been paved by Sidney Webb's Clause 4, was pushed through quickly and painlessly. The coal mines, the gas industry, electricity, the railways, canals, road haulage, airlines, cable and wireless companies, and the Bank of England were all nationalised. The only hitch was iron and steel which were to have an uneasy future of denationalisation and renationalisation. The very success of the overall socialist achievement between 1945 and 1950 was to be a yardstick by which future Labour Governments were to be judged and thus a cause of difficulty within the Labour Party.

The success of the Government was regarded as a mixed blessing by marxist socialists. It had not been necessary to overthrow capitalism to make the welfare state a reality and to nationalise a whole series of industries. Long overdue reforms such as the amelioration of mineworkers' conditions were brought about. The very improvements had contributed to the well-being of the capitalist state.

So much so, that the society improved by Labour was taken over in its entirety by a Conservative government which was to enjoy the main fruits of Labour's achievement, or so it seemed. The Tories made no attempt to unravel the new British socialism. On the contrary, on the foundations laid by Labour they won three general elections, improving their support from a grateful electorate on each occasion.

While the Conservatives followed the broad lines laid

34

down in 1945-51, the Labour opposition now accepted Tory policies. *The Economist* coined the word Butskellism for the two parties' similar approach to home policy, adopted by Butler and Gaitskell. On foreign policy, a bi-partisan approach was also followed.

The decade after the war was the heyday of socialist consensus: consensus in the House of Commons between the parties, and consensus between the wings of the Labour movement. But this consensus was effected in spite of great opposition, primarily because of the weakness of the Left, and the virtual dominance of the reformist, *ad hoc* approach to socialism.

Although this was the era of Aneurin Bevan and the Bevanites, they were locked into a right-wing Labour Party which was scarcely threatened. Bevanites could be regarded as a left-wing ginger group and a force for good, the necessary conscience of the Party. But if they became too obstreperous they could be discarded, expelled or threatened with expulsion.

The Bevanites made their greatest inroads into official Labour policy in foreign affairs, specifically armaments, involving Britain's commitment to NATO. This was the time of British participation in the Korean War, of German re-armament, and of the decision to develop a British hydrogen bomb. In 1954, at the Labour Conference, the question of German re-armament emerged as the most emotive issue of the post-war decade. Opposition by the Left was swelled by many rank and file members who would not normally identify with the Left. Conference approved German re-armament by a whisker. It was not till just after Bevan's death in 1960 that the Party leadership was defeated on a major question of Western defence - the question of unilateral nuclear disarmament.

By then Bevan had anyway become reconciled to the Party line. He had become a member of the Shadow Cabinet and had given up his opposition to the hydrogen bomb, saying that Britain must not go naked into the conference chamber.

Consensus began to come under pressure in the mid-fifties with the advent of new left-wing trade union leaders, in particular Frank Cousins as head of the largest union, the Transport and General Workers' Union. Until then, despite bitter arguments, the Labour Party functioned as one organisation.

Labour had not yet entered the era of what seemed like permanent opposition following electoral defeat in 1959.

Consensus socialism worked on the terms of the Right. The Labour Party was the party of conscience and reform, not of revolution.

The Parliamentary Labour leadership and Labour Members of Parliament were backed by a loyal trade union movement. If Bevanites won six out of seven constituency seats on the NEC in 1952, the overwhelming power of the right-wing trade unions continued to ensure the overall unity of the Labour movement. Conference, the National Executive Committee, the trade unions, MPs, the Shadow Cabinet and the Labour Party in the country kept in step with each other.

The trade unions which had created the Labour Party were able to give it total, decisive support. This was the era of giant figures like Bevin who straddled the movement, bringing Parliamentary Labour and unions together. This was the time when right-wing leaders dominated huge unions and brought stability, with men close to the party leadership like Arthur Deakin, Bevin's successor as secretary of the Transport and General Workers' Union, Will Lawther of the Mineworkers' Union, and Tom Williamson of the General and Municipal Workers. These three could between them muster about a third of the total vote at Conference. They were largely influential in determining who would lead Labour in 1955.

However, the unity of the Labour movement on the terms of the Right carried the seeds of change. The Left wing was not prepared to remain in permanent internal exile, banished from real power, and would make a counter-attack at the end of the decade and in the ensuing eras under Wilson and Callaghan. In contrast, by the late 1970s, the ascendant Left could point a finger to the earlier period and rightly claim that the acceptance of the Left's dominance was the way to a new sort of unity; the Left claimed that they were creating a new consensus.

In any event the unity of the 1950s was a frustrating experience for both Right and Left - for the Left who were without power, and for the Right who had run out of steam after the heady days of the post-war government. Both had to rationalise why Labour was losing support, why three elections were lost with ever worse results. Both were convinced that the problem lay with the other wing of the Party and its influence on the movement, a theme which was to recur in the years ahead. For loss of electoral support would continue to mar Labour's progress both in and out of office.

Unity was put at risk continually over the years, for how

36

could a compromise be accepted on issues such as nuclear armament, entry into Europe, or the extension of party democracy? These were the main issues which were to jeopardise the Party's increasingly vulnerable coalition of interests.

But the issues themselves were only the manifestation of a more fundamental rift. They served as the pretext to challenge what had previously been seen as the natural order of things - the pre-ordained authority of the Right to dictate unity on its terms.

Chapter Seven

ELECTORAL DEFEAT 1959: THE SEEDS OF THE FUTURE

When Labour lost the 1959 election, its third successive general election defeat, many people were questioning whether Labour would ever form a government again, or whether it was doomed to permanent opposition. Labour fortunes and spirits were low. The Conservatives had won 365 seats in the House of Commons; it was then, and would remain, their best post-war result. Even the Thatcher landslide of 339 seats could not match it. By contrast Labour's total was, and remained, the Party's worst post-war showing: 258 seats. In the House of Commons over a hundred seats now separated the two parties.

Little wonder that the Labour Party should suffer a crisis of confidence and that a post-mortem should be initiated. In 1959 as in subsequent years of electoral defeat - in 1970 and 1979 - internal dissent flared. What had gone wrong? Who was to blame? Labour was the party of progress and accordingly should be the party of the future; someone must be to blame for not getting the right message across, or had the Party fought the election on the wrong policies? Then, as in the future, the periods in opposition - with Labour's leading personalities unencumbered by responsibilities of office - were to be used for Labour's internal arguments, which would eventually split the Party in two.

Many of the pointers for the future appeared in the two or three year period following defeat, like the emergence of certain issues as *leitmotifs* which were to recur; like the Right suffering its first major defeat, a new experience at this stage; the Right conducting its first organised campaign, which had previously been the hallmark of left-wing groups, and which proved eminently successful in pulling the Party back on its (right-wing) path; people starting their careers and making names later to become prominent in the Social Democratic

38

story. In retrospect the signposts to the future stand out clearly.

The issues which divided Left and Right at that time were nationalisation and unilateral nuclear disarmament. These and other issues were to return. Certain central issues were chosen by each wing then, as throughout the Party's post-war evolution. Certainly the issues were real; but at the same time, they served as convenient recognisable points around which to rally the fight against the opposing faction and provided symbols of principled commitment with which to identify.

Often the issues were not inherently 'of the Right' or 'of the Left' but only became so through their adoption by one or other faction. A commitment to the European Community, for example, is not essentially a right-wing policy, though it was to become one. Neither was opposition to the EEC of necessity a left-wing attitude. Unilateral nuclear disarmament was not by definition a left-wing policy - many people of all persuasions consider British nuclear weapons to be unnecessary or unacceptable while, conversely, in a world context, a left-wing position in no way deters the Soviet Union from building up its own nuclear capacity. Other issues, however, such as the extension of public ownership, which were in part of Marxist origin, were unambiguously and fundamentally in the tradition of the Left. It was the theme of nationalisation which was to be the focal point of the first battle - a battleground chosen by Hugh Gaitskell himself. As Crossman has written in his diaries, Gaitskell's view was that "it wasn't iron, steel and road haulage, the specific pledges, but the general threat to nationalise six hundred firms which lost us votes."

Within days of the election, a number of leading moderates, including Roy Jenkins, Tony Crosland and Douglas Jay, met Gaitskell at his Hampstead home. They discussed nationalisation and the need to rewrite the party constitution, specifically the relevant Clause 4.

Within a week of Labour's defeat, Jenkins attacked the Party's concentration on nationalisation in the BBC television programme *Panorama* and Douglas Jay argued in print that nationalisation was a liability. 'We must destroy this myth; otherwise we may never win again.'

For Gaitskell and the moderates these initiatives were made against a backcloth of disturbingly contrasting images of the two major parties. The electorate had just given the Conservatives a vote of confidence. It had accepted the campaign slogans of "Life is better with the Conservatives" and "Don't let Labour ruin it". Even for the 40% of people who at the time thought that it did not matter which party was in power, there was no positive reason for switching to Labour.

Furthermore the Labour Party had to compete with a Conservative Party under whose stewardship the country's standard of living had noticeably improved - in marked contrast to Labour whose period of office might be remembered for post-war austerity, hard winters and rationing. Harold Macmillan's "You never had it so good", coupled with the Tories' plan to double the standard of living during the next five years, clearly had electoral appeal.

So the month after the elections, at the annual conference in Blackpool, Gaitskell made a strong plea for modernisation as he saw it. At issue was Labour's out-of-date image, its concern for a class struggle which fought for a type of working man who was fast disappearing, the emphasis on a mechanism for bringing about a better future which was equally dated and irrelevant, namely total nationalisation of the means of production. The solution which Gaitskell proposed was an amendment of the Constitution to reflect the new reality. Gaitskell wanted to dilute Clause 4 to make nationalisation peripheral rather than central to Labour policy - one economic tool in a whole armoury of economic measures, not the Party's principal end. Nationalisation was a means to greater economic accountability and not the end. The Labour Party must demonstrate that it was not wedded to the past, a past symbolised by the advocacy of electorally unpopular nationalisation.

Referring to Clause 4, Gaitskell elaborated: "It implies that the only precise object we have is nationalisation, whereas in fact we have many other Socialist objectives. It implies that we propose to nationalise everything, but do we? Everything? - The whole of light industry, the whole of agriculture, all the shops - every little pub and garage? Of course not. We have long ago come to accept a mixed economy".

Gaitskell's idea was scarcely a cure-all for all the party's ills since it was not a positive step forward but rather the elimination of an unnecessarily negative burden. But neither was it the outrageous attack on the party's *raison d'etre* which some considered it to be. The party's specific pledges did not indicate an uncompromising programme of nationalisation. Gaitskell's attempt to demonstrate to the electorate that the Party was moving with the times was to have an altogether different impact.

Gaitskell's revisionist attempt succeeded only in uniting the party against the moderates' case. Harold Wilson and backbencher Michael Foot, who had just lost his seat in Devonport, claimed that Gaitskell's attempt to revise the Party's Constitution was unnecessarily disruptive. Since Clause 4 was the sentimental core of the Labour Party, little could be gained in creating discord on the subject - and strong feelings were expressed in favour of the retention of the clause. As Wilson said: "We were being asked to take Genesis out of the Bible. You don't have to be a fundamentalist to say that Genesis is a part of the Bible." Foot referred to "... that tiresome controversy ... unleashed by Gaitskell ... On this issue, not Gaitskell, but the Party's rank and file restored the unity so severely damaged." And the Deputy Leader of the Labour Party, Aneurin Bevan, said: "We must not abandon our main case", even though he also stated: "I agree with Hugh - I do not believe in a monolithic society. I do not believe that public ownership should reach down into every piece of economic activity."

For the most part the Labour conference was downright hostile to Gaitskell's attempt to tamper with the Constitution. The resistance the leader encountered in the collision course he had set himself turned out to be fiercer than he had anticipated. Barbara Castle's "It simply won't wash to say that nationalisation is fusty and out of date" was loudly cheered, as was the expression of similar pro-nationalisation sentiments.

The revisionist case was to die, but not without a struggle. Within a few months, in March 1960, the NEC prepared a new twelve-point draft as part of the Constitution, a document which accepted private enterprise as an integral part of the economy. But the matter still roused deep passions among a cross-section of the Party and the NEC finally recognised that the draft would not be passed at the 1960 conference. So, instead of a constitutional amendment, the draft became "a valuable expression of the aims of the Labour Party." To this day, Clause 4, having withstood its greatest challenge, remains intact in Labour Party membership cards.

However, whatever principles of orthodoxy were supported at the Blackpool conference, it is worth noting that the manifesto on which the party was to fight (and win) the next election included no additional measures of nationalisation. The 1964 campaign emphasised economic

41

growth and planning, and only the renationalisation of steel was included in the manifesto.

So nationalisation as an issue was then quietly dropped, but it was to be revived later, after the 1970 and 1979 electoral defeats. Many of the issues raised by Gaitskell in 1959 continued to occupy Labour people up to the time of the Social Democrat exit, and dragged on without a break after the split in the party. What distinguished the time of Gaitskell's challenge from the situation twenty years later was that in 1959 the overriding strength of the Party was still that of the Right. Whatever Gaitskell and the Right suffered as a result of their defeat, it did not fundamentally upset the prevailing balance of the Party, or its apparent unity.

Indeed, the Right's defeat at that time was not caused by the strength of the Left. Rather the raising of the Clause 4 issue united various strands of opinion within the Party. The Left, as a matter of principle, opposed any tampering with this symbolic core of the Constitution. But others, not necessarily allies of the Left, joined it against Gaitskell: the centrists, the old-fashioned trade unionists, loyal and rightist though they were, and the new pragmatists who decided for the sake of socialist appearance to join this principled cause. The role of such pragmatists was to become increasingly prominent over the years.

Perhaps there was also unease at Gaitskell's 'soft' socialism. If socialism did not have a *raison d'etre* distinguishing it fundamentally from the Tories, what remained? Gaitskell's description of the society that Labour was striving for, though desirable, seemed to lack the additional tough dimension that validated socialism. Even the *Sunday Times* (29 November 1959) criticised it. 'Socialist hearers might be forgiven for wondering what war they were being led to fight, what citadel to storm, what enemy to conquer.' Quoting a summary of Gaitskell's principles of Socialism: 'If this is Socialism, what is Radicalism? Support for the 'bottom dog' / Social justice, defined to mean more nearly equal shares of the cake / A classless society / Equality of all races and nations / Personal idealism / The public interest above private interest. Along with Marx and sundry other unwanted objects, Mr Gaitskell has tossed the Webbs and Cole out of the window. What is left can be called Socialism only by virtue of hereditary title.' And finally, the *Sunday Times* referred to the thousands of words spoken by Mr Gaitskell at Blackpool: 'Not one of them was steel ... Where in

Mr Gaitskell's catalogue resides the basic contrast with progressive modern Conservatism?'

Right up to the present this viewpoint is the attacking position adopted by orthodox Socialists. So when the Social Democrats emerged in 1981, they were derided as an alternative Conservative Party, though they themselves had no doubts that they were an alternative to Labour, an alternative radical party.

The modernisation sought in vain by the Labour Party leadership in 1959 was successfully brought about by the Socialist party of a neighbouring European country. That same month, a fortnight before the Blackpool conference, on 13 to 15 November 1959, the Social Democratic Party of West Germany (SPD) met at Bad Godesberg and successfully reached agreement on the Bad Godesberg Programme, a revisionist statement still in force to this day. Its aim was similar to that of the Labour Party moderates: "to move with the times" according to the slogan under which the Bad Godesberg conference met. The German SPD transformed itself from a party representing only the worker into a party with national appeal ('Die Sozialdemokratische Partei ist aus einer Partei der Arbeiterklasse zu einer Partei des Volkes geworden').*

As in Blackpool, much of the discussion centred round the question of nationalisation as a basic aim but it was superseded by a combination of common ownership (Gemeineigentum) and free competition, the latter acknowledged as an "important element" of the economy.

The transformation was an electoral success. In 1966 the SPD joined in a Grand Coalition with the Christlich-Demokratische Union (CDU) as major partner and by 1969 the SPD had become the senior partner in the SPD/FDP (Liberal) coalition, with its own Willy Brandt as Chancellor.

Although Gaitskell and the revisionists had failed where the German SPD succeeded, it could be argued that from the mid-sixties onward both the German and the British parties became parties of government: that they increasingly took on the appearance of 'natural parties of government', and that therefore both had proved successful - the British retention of tradition and the aura of an orthodox past, and the German decision to 'move with the times'.

---

* The SDP has changed from being a party of the working class to a party of the people.

43

Such an argument has flaws. Although both parties did become parties of government, the German route was a steadily ascending share of the vote, whereas the Labour Party's route to success was marked by the opposite. With the exception of 1966, the road from 1951 to 1979 continued to be inexorably downward. At each election a smaller percentage of the electorate cast a positive vote for Labour. Electoral success in subsequent years was only possible for Labour because of the idiosyncrasy of the British electoral system and because the Conservatives' downward slide was even faster than Labour's, the Conservatives losing a third of their support between 1959 and 1974.

The choice the Labour Party faced in 1959, as in 1981, was whether or not to take its place alongside the German SPD and other Social Democratic parties of Europe, as a party of wide appeal, initiating reforms and creating a more just society step by step. For proponents of Social Democracy, this is not Conservatism, nor even diluted Socialism. For David Owen, being a moderate does not imply a lack of radicalism, commitment and passion. "It is the obstinate will to erode by inches which contrasts so sharply with the passionate will to jump by miles...", referred to by Owen in his book *Face the Future*, which is the key to a Social Democracy distinct from both Socialism and Toryism.

If Gaitskell's and Owen's Labour Parties shared a refusal to face the future on social democratic terms, the outcome in each case was very different. In 1959 there was no question but to continue the fight within the Labour Party. The Right was still very much in control and a possible link with the centre, with the Liberals, was rejected out of hand by Gaitskell. One sign of the prevailing Right wind at the Labour Party's Blackpool Conference in November 1959 was the result of the elections onto Labour's National Executive Committee: three hours before he was to take his place as Chairman of the Labour Party, the prominent left-winger, Mr Ian Mikardo lost his place on the National Executive. He was narrowly beaten by an up-and-coming politician whom *The Times* described then as one 'who keeps carefully to the middle of the road': Mr Wedgwood Benn.

Further evidence of a right-wing offensive soon became apparent. The grassroots movement, Campaign for Democratic Socialism, got under way the following year, partly to protect the Party from a new threat - the snowball of unilateral nuclear disarmament - and partly to ensure

44

maximum party support for Gaitskell's moderate leadership *per se*. The politician-to-be - for he was not yet in the House of Commons - most closely and dynamically linked with the CDS was Bill Rodgers.

Chapter Eight

CONFERENCE AND PARLIAMENTARY LABOUR PARTY: TRIAL SEPARATION 1960-1

In many ways the famous Clause 4 controversy was a non-event. No resolution had been made, no vote taken, no formal defeat inflicted. However, the Labour Party had failed to take the opportunity to modernise, to become a national party on the German SPD Bad Godesberg model, and to move away from a narrow working class concept of the Party. This failure was to plague it over the years, contributing considerably to the continuous decline in electoral support. But meanwhile a new conflict rocked the Labour Party and raised, for the first time, some fundamental questions which with the passage of the years would become important in the division of the movement into Labour and Social Democracy.

For the very first time, the Labour leadership was formally defeated on a major issue of policy. In October 1960, Conference approved motions for unilateral nuclear disarmament, which not only split the movement down the middle but, more important, made the Parliamentary Labour Party and Conference go separate ways, the PLP rejecting the authority of Conference.

At the 1960 Conference Gaitskell had given notice before the vote was taken that "there are some of us, Mr Chairman, who will fight and fight and fight again to save the Party we love. We will fight and fight and fight again to bring back sanity and honesty and dignity, so that our Party with its great past may retain its glory and its greatness." By this Gaitskell had meant not only that he would fight to reverse the decision but that the PLP would act independently and would not accept the authority of Conference if Conference voted for unilateralism. Given the block union votes already mandated, it was known that the official line would be defeated. On four separate votes, this proved to be the case.

The defence policy approved by the NEC, the TUC General Council and the PLP was rejected by 297,000 votes.

46

By just 43,000 votes Frank Cousins' motion on behalf of the Transport and General Workers' Union, calling for a "complete rejection of any defence policy based on the threat of the use of strategic or tactical nuclear weapons" was carried.

By 407,000 votes, Conference voted for the Amalgamated Engineering Union motion in favour of the "unilateral renunciation of the testing, manufacture, stock piling and basing of all nuclear weapons in Great Britain."

A motion from the Woodworkers, supporting the official defence policy and declaring that Britain's membership of NATO was imperative, was defeated by 332,000 votes.

The margins separating the victors from the vanquished were very small; they ranged from less than one per cent to a maximum of under seven percent of the total six and a half million votes at Scarborough. With such close results the issues could as easily have been decided the other way.

Gaitskell's impassioned speech had convinced as many uncommitted votes as possible, but the bulk of the votes were previously mandated and delegates were thus impervious to argument. The net result was that a major policy statement on defence did not gain the backing of Conference.

For Gaitskell the dilemma was clear: the conflicting allegiance of Labour's MPs to the Labour movement and to the electorate. This was to become a fundamental issue and eventually a breaking point for many. The question revolved round accountability - but to whom? To the Labour Party or to the nation? Was the object internal Party democracy or a more broadly based democracy?

Gaitskell put it this way: "It is not the end of the problem because Labour MPs will have to consider what they do in the House of Commons. What do you expect of them? You know how they voted in June - overwhelmingly for the policy statement. It is not in dispute that the vast majority of Labour MPs are utterly opposed to unilateralism and neutralism. What do you expect them to do? To change their minds overnight, to go back on the pledges they gave to the people who elected them in their constituencies? And supposing they do that. Supposing all of us, like well-behaved sheep, were to follow suddenly the policies of unilateralism and neutralism - what kind of impression will this make on the British people? I do not believe the Labour MPs are prepared to act as time servers."

For the committed Left it was also the occasion to seek a

new leader. Konni Zilliacus said: "Mr Gaitskell's arrogance and fanaticism and his hydrogen bomb strategy mean that he is not fit to lead the party and will have to go." Zilliacus's criterion was willingness to accept Conference decisions. For Gaitskell, the leadership question, as also the matter of Party policies, was ultimately the prerogative of the PLP. "Let me repeat what Shinwell said - the place to decide the leadership of the party is not here but in the Parliamentary Labour Party. I would not wish for one day to remain a leader who had lost the confidence of his colleagues in Parliament." It was this very issue of who should elect the leader which, almost exactly twenty years later, was to be the signal for the fragmentation of the party.

In January 1981, at Wembley, the Labour Party finalised its new procedure for electing its leader. The PLP was given a minority vote of 30%, while the trade unions had 40% and the constituency Labour parties the other 30%. The next day the Council of Social Democracy was in existence and two months later the Social Democratic Party.

The issue of unilateralism itself was also raised again twenty years later. As in 1960, the attempt to move the party to unilateralism was backed by a variety of groups. In 1960, members of the Campaign for Nuclear Disarmament, a movement which enjoyed growing popular appeal, were often members of the Labour Party. Some saw support as a way of winning votes. Others on the Left, as a means of dislodging right-wing leadership. All were united in voting against the official line. But for Gaitskell, those who attacked the Party's defence policy included people opposed to NATO and the American alliance, some who were neutralist and others who were sympathetic to the Soviet Union and to Communism. He reminded the conference of sixty resolutions for withdrawal from NATO: "Do you think we can become overnight the pacifist, unilateralist and fellow travellers that other people are?" So it was that Gaitskell and the overwhelmingly right-wing Labour PLP rejected 1960 Scarborough Party Conference decisions and followed their own Westminster line of multilateralism and adherence to NATO and the American alliance. Indeed, those in Parliament who followed the unilateralist line were the ones who became the rebels, not vice versa. In the end the remaining five unilateralist diehards in the Commons were deprived of the whip.

When Harold Wilson challenged Gaitskell for the leadership shortly afterwards, it was not because he was a unilateralist. Rather he presented himself as a candidate who would bring unity. It was the first time that an incumbent Labour leader had been challenged in this way. Gaitskell was overwhelmingly returned, and George Brown took the deputy leadership made vacant by the death of Aneurin Bevan. The Right's position was doubly re-affirmed.

Although there had been a rift between Conference and the Parliamentary Labour Party, the latter continued to follow its own policies regardless. This was only possible because the National Executive Committee was prepared to back it all the way. An essential difference between 1961 and 1981 was that in 1961 the NEC was still a right-wing body, working closely with the PLP. Whatever the differences, there was mutual trust and understanding. Thus, the NEC bent over backwards not to allow the rather uncompromising resolution passed by Conference to stand in isolation. This had been approved on a two-to-one basis: "While acknowledging that the day-to-day tactics in Parliament must be the job of the Parliamentary party, this conference declares that Labour policy is decided by the party conference, which is the final authority."

However the NEC qualified this, thereby turning the resolution on its head: "The National Executive Committee does not wish to oppose the composite resolution so long as it is clearly understood by everybody that it involves no change in the long-established principles which have governed the relationships of the party conference, the National Executive Committee and the Parliamentary Party - so long as it is clearly understood that nobody at all has the power to instruct, control or dictate to the Parliamentary Labour Party on the way it carries out its responsibilities."

So Gaitskell could afford to go his own way. Priority could be given to maintaining a show of consistency to the electorate. The main aim - to win the next election - could still be pursued single-mindedly.

For all that, the condition of the Labour Party was not a comfortable one. For the first time the trade union block vote had been used against its traditional allies and, as the *Sunday Times'* political correspondent, James Margach wrote at the week-end following the Scarborough conference: 'In the industrial wing the old balances are rapidly shifting. The rising power of the Left-wing unions, headed by Mr Cousins, has placed the political Left very much in the ascendency. '

Margach spoke of the suicide of Labour, and saw two rival Labour parties emerging: "Some honest brokers", he wrote, "believe that the Labour movement will never again become a powerful political force until the Left hives off from the main body - or until the Centre-to-Right breaks from a Left-dominated party."

Twenty years later, yes. For the moment, Gaitskell's immediate "fight and fight and fight" was only beginning. Who would be fighting with him?

Chapter Nine

CAMPAIGN FOR DEMOCRATIC SOCIALISM: MODEL FOR THE FUTURE

It is a curious fact that up to this stage in the evolution of the Labour Party, the only organised pressure groups inside the Party were left-wing. Perhaps this is because until 1960, in spite of vocal disputes, the Right had been firmly in charge. Perhaps the Left had been forced to create 'parties within the party' precisely because it was weak. The Keep Left Group, Tribune, Victory for Socialism, were left-wing voices in a right-wing Labour Party.

Now, for the first time, the Right was under sufficient pressure to feel threatened. Even before the defeat at Scarborough, soon after the "what kind of a Labour party do we want?" disputes at Blackpool, the Right began to group with the intention of influencing the answer.

One of the first manifestations from the young blood on the Right came within two months of the Blackpool conference. On 3 February 1960, fifteen parliamentary candidates wrote to Gaitskell pledging their support: "We regard your leadership as settled and look to you to lead Labour back to power again". Signatories not yet in the House of Commons included Shirley Williams, Dick Taverne, Bill Rodgers, Merlyn Rees and Bryan Magee. Rodgers, General Secretary of the Fabian Society from 1953 to 1960, and parliamentary candidate in Bristol West in 1957, was the prime mover behind the letter.

Rodgers was also one of the prime movers in the Campaign for Democratic Socialism. In 1960 like-minded Labour people were meeting: in London, Rodgers, Taverne, Michael Shanks and others; in Oxford, city alderman, Frank Pickstock, Philip Williams, fellow of Nuffield College, and Brian Walden began to plan a grassroots campaign to win back a Labour Party which seemed to be slipping away from them.

51

The aim was to mobilise support in the constituencies, provide information and arguments for the Right's policies and offset the continuous flow of left-wing propaganda which had become traditional, so that trade unionists, Parliamentary and constituency Labour Parties should unite behind Gaitskell.

The Oxford/London group had access to the highest echelons around Gaitskell, and met in June 1960 to start the ball rolling. The meeting upstairs at the Prince of Wales in Chelsea included about twenty people, all the leading Gaitskellites. Douglas Jay, Roy Jenkins, Patrick Gordon Walker, Crosland, and Pickstock but not Gaitskell.

Although there was an intimate connection with the leading Gaitskellites, this was not publicised. The so-called Hampstead set around Gaitskell had a somewhat elitist image which, it was felt, would be detrimental. Still, if the aim was for grassroots to talk to grassroots, to demonstrate rank-and-file support for the leadership, this was not immediately evident at the Prince of Wales.

Pickstock recalls that the meeting seemed to be concentrating on what sort of a letter to write to *The Times*. He was horrified. Few of the people present had any organising experience at local level. 'We set up a small working committee. Bill Rodgers became Chairman, Dick Taverne Treasurer, I was Secretary and Denis Howell looked after publicity. I said £200 would keep us going till the October conference. We passed the hat round and started.'

Initially Pickstock with a part-time secretary operated from his home, with the immediate task of writing a manifesto. After his first draft, the manifesto developed its own life. Draft followed draft, with Crosland and Philip Williams getting very involved in the wording. 'We ran to 36 drafts.'

It also became clear that unilateral nuclear disarmament was going to be the issue at Scarborough. 'We assumed Gaitskell would lose. At the same time we felt this was a good issue to fight. We could turn the tide back. So just as the Left chose 'Europe' later, as a convenient battleground, we chose nuclear disarmament. Where previously it had just been one of the issues, after Scarborough it became the issue on which we could beat the Left.' It was also the issue to heal the wounds on the Right caused by the Clause 4 controversy. For opposition to unilateralism, symbolising the much broader question of the party's fundamental attitude to NATO and the American alliance, could unite the broad span of moderates.

Immediately after the expected defeat, so narrowly inflicted by the trade union block votes, a new opening paragraph was added and the text of the manifesto released. It now appealed for resistance to and reversal of "the present disastrous trend towards unilateralism and neutralism" and for a modern classless Labour Party in Gaitskell's image. The manifesto, signed by twenty-six members of the Party from the originial steering group and from constituency Labour parties and union representatives from the regions, was sent out to a carefully selected mailing list. At the ensuing press conference, Rodgers, harking back to Gaitskell's fighting speech thirteen days before, called for a victory for sanity. Briefly, the Campaign became known under that name: 'Victory for Sanity'. But it was as the 'Campaign for Democratic Socialism' that it earned its honourable mention in the history books. It is worth considering for a moment the curious importance given to labels of this sort. In 1960, 'Democratic Socialism' was interchangeable with 'Social Democracy'. The Campaign for Democratic Socialism of 1960 was the direct precursor of the Social Democratic Party of 1981.

Yet somewhere in the interim period, the two labels developed separate meanings. Today, those on the Left make the distinction between a democratic socialism which aims to change society, creating a new social system, and social democracy which initiates individual progressive measures but basically leaves the system as it is and is therefore inadequate. These distinctions become even more curious when one considers that the Social Democratic Federation (SDF), a co-founder of the Labour Party, was a marxist body.

CDS was highly successful. It was very well organised. Much of the credit for this went to Rodgers and Pickstock. Though *Tribune* referred to CDS as a "squalid little conspiracy", it generally received an excellent press. Messages of support flowed in, including one from Lord Attlee, who was to become the Campaign's President some months later. It helped the Party swing back to its former posture, unambiguously on the Right.

The unilateralist tide was stemmed. Gaitskell was re-elected leader by a two-to-one majority against Harold Wilson. The TUC conference in September 1961 voted three to one for Gaitskell's 'Policy for Peace'. Cousin's union, the TGWU, was the only one of the big six unions to oppose it. The following month at Blackpool, at the annual party conference, the dispute was finally settled. The official defence policy was approved, 4,526,000 votes for and 1,756,000 against; the unilateralist motion was rejected seven to one. Where the year before the unilateralists had won on a tiny margin, Gaitskell had now won decisively.

When the Labour Party won the General Election of 1964, CDS felt that this was the moment to bow out. It had helped consolidate the Party on its terms and send it united to the polls. In October 1964, resting on its laurels, CDS proclaimed its own dissolution.

CDS was the first organised fight of the Right and in many ways became the model used for subsequent campaigns by the Labour Right. There are many similarities with Campaign for Labour Victory founded in 1977, out of which the Social Democratic Party subsequently evolved. Both CDS and the CLV had a four-year life-span. Both operated at grassroots level to influence the climate of opinion within the Party. But there was a fundamental difference. Where in 1960 the Party was still a party of the Right with the NEC, the trade union leadership and the PLP basically united, by 1977 the Party was of the Left. The Campaign for Labour Victory had set itself a far tougher task.

In fact, although the Campaign for Democratic Socialism saw all its aims realised, the extent to which success actually stemmed from the Campaign has been questioned. It must be said at once that the Campaign was efficient. Through a network in constituency Labour parties and union branches, good contact was maintained. Moderates for the first time felt supported and well-briefed. It gave them a feeling that they were not fighting in isolation.

At the same time, there was a strong wish for unity, the Labour movement having been shaken by its divisions. Once Gaitskell had been re-elected, unity meant unity on Gaitskell's terms. It required but a modest swing in the trade unions to bring the consensus behind official defence policy and behind Gaitskell. Undoubtedly the CDS must have contributed to the process of change.

Gaitskell himself, through his strong leadership and through his personal campaigning, was a major influence in convincing all but his most determined enemies. But ultimately Labour people recognised that two separate sets of policies would undermine Labour's position at the next election, and that unity was essential for electoral victory.

That having been said, the Campaign for Democratic

Socialism functioned well, and served as a model for the future. Taverne and Rodgers were soon to enter the House of Commons and subsequently to play important roles in the gestation and foundation of the Social Democratic Party. As in 1960 so in 1981, the Right selected its issue and fought its battle round it. With one major difference, however: in 1960 Rodgers and his colleagues made the choice of attempting a straight victory inside the Party. By 1981 Rodgers and his associates knew that defeat within the Party was necessary to free them for a new political existence outside the Party.

PART III

THE LABOUR PARTY UNDER NEW MANAGEMENT: SOCIAL DEMOCRACY UNDER PRESSURE

Chapter Ten

THE WILSON YEARS

Under New Management

To understand how the SDP could emerge in 1981 and
blossom into a legitimate new party, it is necessary to look
more closely at the events of the years when Harold Wilson
was Prime Minister.

Harold Wilson may have talked disparagingly of the
thirteen wasted years under the Conservatives (1951-1964),
but how will history judge his own thirteen years as leader of
the Labour Party (1963-1976)? Harold Wilson, the man who
was greeted with the highest hopes both by his country and his
party, finally handed over the reins of power of his own accord,
but with few tears shed for him. The country which he had
taken over sound and stable, had become the sick country of
Europe, economically weak, politically divided and difficult to
govern. The united party which he had inherited was on the
way to fragmentation.

In 1964, when Wilson led the Labour Party to victory at
the polls, the country was ready for a change of government.
Labour only won by a handful of seats, although the
Conservatives had had their Profumo debacle and had
generally run out of steam; but Wilson's victory was hailed
with a good measure of optimism.

Wilson's image was enhanced by the contrast with the
Oppositions's leadership - first with Prime Minister Harold
Macmillan, at the end of his tenure of office, the faded
SuperMac of Vicky cartoons, and soon after with what
appeared to be another joke figure from a bygone age:
aristocratic Sir Alec Douglas Home. Against such political
opponents, Wilson appeared the man of today, and, what is
more, of tomorrow.

Harold Wilson, of Northern accent and ever present
pipe, was clever. He had, at 31, been the youngest cabinet
minister in Attlee's government, and at 48 was the youngest

prime minister since William Pitt. He was of the same generation as President Kennedy of the United States. Similarly charismatic, dynamic, visionary, his words struck a sympathetic chord in the country: "We are re-defining and we are re-stating our socialism in terms of the scientific revolution . . . The Britain that is going to be forged in the white heat of this revolution will be no place for restrictive practices or out-dated methods on either side of industry."

But the scientific revolution never took place; restrictive practices and trade union stoppages flourished and the dramatic improvement in management methods failed to materialise. The promises turned out to be empty. Where under the Tories there had been modest growth, stability and more or less full employment, under Wilson the country seemed to drift from crisis to crisis. What use acknowledged cleverness, when high inflation and unemployment were becoming features of our way of life. By the time Wilson resigned as Prime Minister in 1976, inflation had peaked at an unprecedented 26.9%, and unemployment was climbing to its then post-war peak of over one and a half million.

On the way, a whole series of promises went unfulfilled and the man who was always available to newsmen became paranoid about the media; for the Rhodesian crisis was not resolved in a matter of weeks; the pound *was* devalued; the Social Contract between Labour Government and the trade unions failed. The media had not invented these. The gap between utterance and performance widened and credibility dwindled.

Wilson's real success was in winning elections - four out of five. But it was his style of leadership that was so crucial over the longer term. It is ironic that the man who saw his mission as party leader in the achievement of unity, no matter what the cost, was the man who presided while it accelerated toward rupture.

By his own yardstick of keeping the Party together, Wilson failed. Within a mere dozen years, the Labour Party which he had taken over as a united social democratic party had shifted violently to the left and the shift had transformed it into a deeply divided party, or more like two opposing parties, trapped under one label. Why should Labour be splitting? Why on the terms of the Left? And why had it happened so fast?

Perhaps, like happiness, unity evaporates if you seek it for its own sake. There is little use bridging over the widening cracks if the bridge is a *trompe l'oeil*, more cosmetic than functional. Wilson's supporters would probably have agreed that he was the man to keep the party together if any man could. His many critics would say that his attempts to keep the party together were to the detriment of the country. To his critics, it was clear that the cost was too high. But in any event he failed.

Wilson's leadership of the Labour Party was in total contrast to Gaitskell's. Perhaps it was Gaitskell's example which made Wilson determine he would not run the same risk of splitting the party. Why confront the party with issues of principle which split it in half? What use the needless creation of strife? To Wilson, Gaitskell's unsuccessful fight against the Clause 4 'theology' was a lesson in how not to lead.

Wilson had already put himself forward as Party leader during Gaitskell's lifetime - the first time an incumbent leader had been challenged for the job. In 1960 Wilson campaigned as the 'unity' candidate, as John Silkin did more recently in the 1981 contest for Deputy Leader of the Labour Party. Neither won.

By the time Wilson was elected, following the death of Hugh Gaitskell in January 1963, the Party had anyway closed ranks. It smelt electoral victory, and although Gaitskell's personal hostility toward the European idea had deeply disappointed his social democratic followers, it had, paradoxically, unified the party. Having been elected, Wilson's first mandate, as he put it, was to maintain the unity of the party that Hugh Gaitskell had handed on three weeks before.

If he was chosen to lead, it was in spite of his left-wing reputation in the party. According to the composition of the Party at that time, George Brown, caretaker leader of three weeks, or even the third candidate, Jim Callaghan, should have become leader. Wilson won because he was seen as the most able of the three. His left-wing credentials were not seen as sufficient threat in a Gaitskellite party and this view was borne out by his second mandate to continue those policies worked out under Gaitskell's leadership.

In fact Wilson, the Left's own candidate and favourite of the constituency parties, did indeed go on to pursue the middle-of-the-road, progressive policies of his predecessor. It was his interpretation of the leader's role rather than policies which accelerated the drift to the left. His style was that of party manager, not of emotional leader, responding to pressures rather than creating them. He substituted expedient action for visionary goals, a style which earned Wilson the label 'pragmatic' and taught the man in the street a new word. Doing what the party seemed to want, leading from behind, as if to say: "These are the members of my party. I must follow them. I am the leader."

This interpretation of leadership might be considered more democratic than Gaitskell's style, but it could also be regarded as less principled, in the sense that Wilson's principles did not need to be nailed to the mast, for it seemed that almost no principle was important enough to fight for to the bitter end. Goals as important as Britain's membership of the European Community, or getting trade union legislation right, could change according to the pressures within the party, the pressures from Left or Right, whether Labour was in government or in opposition. The criterion was not to be: what is right for the country is right for the Party, but rather what is right for the Party has to be right for the country.

Wilson's style has left its mark particularly on the right wing of Labour. Principles have been watered down to the point where some Labour MPs no longer care enough to fight for them: unilateral or multilateral disarmament - an argument can be made either way; staying in the Common Market or not - either standpoint can be defended; trade union block votes to help select the Party leader may not be ideal but we can live with that. Though a second chamber is useful, and reform of the House of Lords even better, doing away with it is not important enough to be of real concern. And so it goes on. The breaking point for many MPs vanished to a distant horizon.

The central issue which has come to dominate all others is the health of the Party. The sicker it became, the greater the need to play the party game; the further it drifted leftward, the more leftist noises needed to be made, not least of all by those on the right of the Party.

Credentials became important. Those on the left had no problem. In an era where they were making the running, they did not need to prove them. Those on the right had to be seen to be more progressive, more socialist, merely to occupy the new centre. Who would have thought that things would go so far that, by the end of the seventies, the centre of the party would be represented by Michael Foot, the man who to an earlier generation had symbolised the extreme Left.

If the Party under Wilson's leadership had shifted its axis of acceptability leftwards, Wilson's influence was clearly only one factor in the process. Nor had this been his intention. As Bernard Crick has commented, Harold Wilson was the weakest British prime minister if the criterion is the ability to carry out a premeditated intention.

Wilson began his premiership intending to be even-handed, to favour neither Left nor Right. But that, paradoxically, in itself meant a swing to the left. Having inherited from Gaitskell a shadow cabinet composed of right-wing Labour people, his first action on winning the 1964 General Election was to bring into his cabinet a number of strong left-wingers. Whatever his reasons, the result was a block of left-wing ministers in the Cabinet, a constellation which would have been unlikely under Gaitskell. So Frank Cousins, the militant left-wing Secretary of the Transport and General Workers' Union, became Minister of Technology, Barbara Castle, Minister of Overseas Development and Anthony Greenwood, Colonial Secretary.

In fact, in the first two years of government, Wilson could justifiably congratulate himself. Despite a majority in the House of Commons which could be counted on the fingers of one hand, his government conducted its affairs as if it had an adequate majority. Indeed, Wilson thrived on adversity, and potential dissidents in the House or in the Labour movement were not ready to threaten the new government. After thirteen years in the wilderness the possession of power and influence was too precious, and Wilson was able to play on this. 1964 to 1966 was still an era of balance within the Party; a balance achieved on the terms of the Right.

In 1966, when Wilson rightly assessed that his electoral chances were good, he went to the country. This time he won handsomely, with a substantial working majority.

The Unions Provoked

With his unsuccessful attempt to curb trade union power, Wilson's troubles really began. Had he been successful, it is possible that the Labour Party would have evolved quite differently, that Wilson's 'even-handed' approach would have worked, and that Left and Right would have continued to be broadly balanced within the Party. As it was, the unions became less controllable and exerted unprecedented influence on the movement.

As paymasters, as the voice of the working man, and as wielders of block votes at the annual conference, the unions personified the Labour Party's *raison d'etre*, which is why the conflict between Wilson and the unions was so divisive. The trade unions now became increasingly militant. Their vote dominated Annual Conference and the National Executive Committee. The traditionally right-wing unions had been stung into left-wing actions. The era of right-wing unions was over.

Wilson had already given advance warning that the trade unions would need to play their part in his economic programme. In the drive toward industrial modernisation and economic success, "there is no room for Luddites in the Socialist Party". His government's difficulties reinforced Wilson's determination to take action. However, the Prime Minister noted for his pragmatic approach and for his wish to maintain unity, by the actions he took merely succeeded in exacerbating trade union militancy and party divisions.

Within six weeks of being hailed the victor of the 1966 election, Wilson found himself facing a protracted seamen's strike. The seven-week stoppage posed an increasing threat to his economic strategy, as he saw exports fall and the pound slip on the foreign exchanges. His personal appeals to the seamen to return to work went unheeded. Wilson attacked the strike as Communist-inspired and described it as "against the state, against the community."

As the administration floundered, confronted by a stream of economic crises, the election slogan of 1966 - "You know Labour government works" - began to look somewhat ill-founded. In the choice between deflation and devaluation, Labour chose deflation, but was forced into devaluation as well, after endless protestations that devaluation was not the way out of the crisis. As James Callaghan, then Chancellor of the Exchequer, stated: "Those who advocate devaluation are calling for a reduction in the wage levels and the real wage standards of every member of the working class of this country."

And that is what the battle was about. Trade unions, who saw their standards of living threatened, were, at the same time, being given less bargaining power over their pay, for as the crisis deepened, the Government introduced legislation to curb wage increases. In the summer of 1966 a six-month wage freeze was imposed with a period of severe wage restraint to follow. At the same time, the Government deflated, hitting living standards by putting up the cost of cigarettes and spirits, by restricting foreign holiday expenditure to £50 a year, and by tougher hire purchase regulations. Finally, after wage freeze and wage restraint and deflation, devaluation followed as well. Wilson broadcast to the nation: "This does not mean that the pound in your pocket has been devalued."

Within two months, more unpalatable medicine was in store for the population: no more free milk for children in secondary schools, housing and road-building programmes cut, medical prescriptions to be paid for, dental treatment to cost more, the raising of the school leaving age from fifteen to sixteen postponed by two years from 1971 to 1973.

Within another two months, March 1968, with Roy Jenkins now replacing Callaghan as Chancellor of the Exchequer, a further dose was inflicted - this time in the wake of an international monetary crisis. Cigarettes and spirits went up again. So did petrol, and the car tax rose to £25. Jenkins, who is presented by the Social Democratic Party as the best Chancellor since the war, promised only "a stiff budget followed by two years of hard slog."

Little wonder that there was widespread unease in the Labour movement and particularly amongst trade unions. This was scarcely a Socialist utopia, nor even the modest economic growth which they had looked forward to under a Labour government whose leader promised new efficiency and success compared with earlier Tory administrations.

Why did a Cabinet of such high calibre, which included not only Wilson but some of the most impressive brains in British politics - Crossman, Crosland, Jenkins and Healey - have so much difficulty in steering the country? Where was the correlation between cerebral excellence and effective government?

The greater the economic problem, the more disquiet in the party. The more pressure was exerted to keep the trade unions in line to help the economy, the more the unions resisted. By now, new left-wing leaders had risen to the top. Hugh Scanlon had become leader of the Engineers' Union (1967). In 1969 Jack Jones had taken over as Secretary of the Transport and General Workers' Union. Up till then the TGWU had again been led by the militant Frank Cousins who had resigned from Wilson's Government within two years of joining, one of the early opponents of the Government's measures restricting free collective bargaining.

Now, in 1968, the Trade Union Congress voted eight to one against the official wages policy of the Government. The Labour Party Conference shortly afterwards, with the contribution of the trade union block of votes, likewise gave the policy its thumbs down, five to one against.

Wilson's incomes policy was also threatened by a series of strikes which were doubtless multiplying as a result of that policy. Each year the number of working days lost increased: in 1966 2.4 million; in 1967 2.8 million; in 1968 4.7 million; in 1969 6.8 million. (This trend was to continue under Heath's Government, reaching a peak of 23.9 million in 1972).

It was in the middle of that graph's upward curve that the Government decided that action was called for. That attempt to curb trade union power, failing as it did, affected more than anything else future relationships between Government and unions and between the different sections within the Labour Party. Unlike his predecessor Gaitskell who, having failed to carry the day, promised to fight and fight and fight again, Wilson retreated from the battle. Indeed he was later to join sides with the adversary, the trade union movement.

In January 1969, Wilson made his pitch on the issue of strikes. He had become convinced that these were damaging not only to the economy but also to the Labour Party. He was supported in his view by opinion polls which consistently showed a high percentage of the public hostile to trade union strikes and practices. Wilson proposed to introduce legislation on the basis of a White Paper, 'In Place of Strife' and he went well beyond the Government's own Donovan Commission recommendations, which, after a three-year investigation, had basically come out in favour of more of the same, concentrating on the improvement of bargaining procedures without new legislation. Wilson, together with his left-wing Employment Secretary, Barbara Castle, sought to legislate.

'In Place of Strife' included three penal proposals. The first was that there should be a conciliation or cooling-off period of twenty-eight days in certain disputes before a strike became effective; the second, that members of the trade unions involved in certain disputes should be ballotted; and third that, in the case of inter-union disputes, a solution could, in the final resort, be imposed by the relevant minister. Legal sanctions would be available to enforce the new measures.

To observers with no particular axe to grind, these proposals appeared neither far-reaching, nor repressive, nor controversial. They were merely rules in the industrial relations game which sought to ensure that the strike card was played only after due consideration and democratic consultation. But the proposals *were* controversial, for they were interpreted as an attack on the trade unions.

That a Labour Government should be attacking the unions was a blow. That Barbara Castle, the 'bonny fighter' and champion of the workers, should now be waging a struggle against them was an added blow and scarcely credible to the faithful. The unions were not alone in opposing the proposals; various factions of the Labour movement also came out against them. As the White Paper was debated within the movement, it became clear that it was going to have a rough passage. Labour back-benchers abstained or voted against the measures. The NEC voted sixteen to five against, with Cabinet Minister Callaghan included in the majority. A TUC congress overwhelmingly opposed the proposed legislation. The Cabinet split. As late as two weeks before defeat, Wilson was still fighting - comparing the trade unions with the oldest profession, in that both enjoyed power without responsibility. But with chief whip Robert Mellish's message that the bill had no chance in the House of Commons, Wilson and Castle had to bow to the wind. A substitute formula was quickly cobbled together: the TUC would do its best to promote responsible union behaviour. The formula had no teeth and was to prove as ineffective as it appeared at the time. After five months the strife-generating 'In Place of Strife' was dead.

Each crisis in the Labour Party tends to be described as 'The worst since 1931'. The 'In Place of Strife' dispute was so described and indeed, it did affect the party's development. For where the 1964 to 1966 Labour administration could be broadly described as a social democratic administration, thereafter the swing to the left changed the hallmark of the party in a way which neither those inside nor outside the party could ignore.

Wilson failed in two ways - by not getting the economy right and by not succeeding in reforming the trade unions. One affected the other: economic problems were heightened by trade union militancy and trade unions were militant because the economic problems were biting into their standard of living.

Like Gaitskell, whose example he wished to avoid, Wilson managed to unite the party on an emotional issue - against what he was trying to achieve. With Clause 4, Gaitskell attacked the sentimental core of the party which ran deeper than left-wing and right-wing factions. Wilson tackling the unions found himself in a similar position, fighting both

Left and Right, opposed by a broad spectrum of the movement. He too had touched a Labour Party nerve end. The fact that in both cases the leaders were fighting to modernise the movement, and were pursuing reforms which were electorally popular, did not help.

If Wilson failed, so had the predominantly right-wing Government and Parliamentary Labour Party. Had Callaghan not lent his weight to the unions, had there been a collective will to push the modest union reforms through onto the statute book, modernisation might have overcome difficulties and won the day. But, as Wilson is reported to have said, "the Cabinet turned yellow" *, and too many in the House withheld their votes.

The Labour government which was to have been such a contrast to tired Conservative government had done little more than survive, tacking into the economic winds. Labour only just lost the 1970 General Election, but lose they did. Now the recriminations and the infighting could begin without fear of embarrassing a Labour Party in government.

In Opposition Again

It would be difficult to exaggerate the low morale of the party at this point. Disillusion was the overriding emotion. The constituency party workers, in particular, felt betrayed. The disparity between the aspirations and the reality of Labour's achievements in power seemed to many grotesque. It was accepted by the party faithful that there had been achievements, notably social reforms - divorce had been made easier, homosexual relations between consenting adults were no longer criminal, capital punishment abolished, theatre censorship had been ended and, Wilson's own favourite, the University of the Air, popularly known as the Open University, was established. But for those hungry for sweeping changes in society, these and other worthwhile reforms were not compensation enough to offset an unsuccessful, crisis-ridden, monetarist, pragmatic Wilson Government.

The election post-mortem was perhaps more like a kangaroo court. The guilt of the Government was established

---

* From essay by Paul Johnson 'Farewell to the Labour Party' in *Right Turn*, edited by Patrick Cormack, published by Leo Cooper, 1978

before the proceedings began. It was merely necessary to ensure that no future Labour government could betray the movement's trust. Above all, the party at large felt that its views must be heeded. It represented the conscience of the movement which had been systematically ignored. Party activists could point to Conference decisions which had been ignored on repeated occasions. Wilson, their own left-wing choice, who had always spoken up for the primacy of Conference when Gaitskell was leader, had not noticeably changed government policy after conceding no less than thirteen major Conference defeats between 1966 and 1969.

The outgoing Labour Government had been discredited, but Wilson nevertheless retained his place, appearing at this point as the only man to lead, straddling left and right wings, and still admired in the party.

In the trade unions, in Parliament, at Conference, and on the National Executive Committee (more powerful when Labour is in opposition), movement was leftwards. The right-wing policies of the old government having been found wanting, the party tide had turned. Left-wing policies and ideas were gaining acceptance. The old social democratic wing was too much on the defensive to put up a concerted fight for its own views - except on entry into the European Community where, though the Right was in the minority in the Party, it did fight.

Nationalisation, which Gaitskell had, amid so much noise, tried to consign to the waste-paper basket and which had been relegated quietly and unobtrusively by Wilson, was now back on the table. Successive conferences voted for public ownership of banking, insurance, building societies, finance houses, the building industry, road haulage, shipbuilding and ship repairing.

With Tony Benn chairing the NEC's Home Policy Committee review of Party policy, 'Labour's Programme for Britain' incorporated extensive nationalisation, and renationalisation where the Conservatives had denationalised. By 1973 the Programme proposals included the take-over of twenty-five of Britain's largest profitable companies. The manifesto on which the Party fought the 1974 election, though subsequently a little diluted, was the most radical since 1945.

In the meantime the left-wing group of Tribune MPs published 'Labour - Party or Puppet?', co-authored by Frank Allaun, Ian Mikardo and Jim Sillars (now of the Scottish Nationalists). This was one of the earliest initiatives seeking to

69

tie the Parliamentary Labour Party to the movement and make it more accountable to Conference and the Labour Party as a whole. From this tiny acorn was to grow the oak of the final party democracy conflict.

Proposals included changes to the composition of the NEC: constituency parties would have the right to elect twelve instead of seven representatives, six MPs and six rank and file. The Women's Section was to be cut from five to one. The Deputy Leader's job would be dispensed with and his seat would therefore disappear. Had these changes been implemented, one of the consequences would have been to avoid the Benn/Healey/Silkin contest in 1981, but the immediate intention was clearly to strengthen the Left's control.

The leader of the party was to be elected by Conference as a whole. Parliamentary candidates were to be selected by activists rather than the constituency membership. Burke's contention that MPs should be accountable to their consciences rather than be mandated was considered outdated: "We do not live in Burke's world any more, and it is time the Parliamentary Party understood that the aristocratic concepts which ruled these islands in the eighteenth century are unfitted for a modern democracy." Thus MPs were to sign an undertaking to carry out the party programme. Conference would be the final authority for that programme. Although none of the Tribune Group's recommendations survived in this form, their spirit did.

The Tribune Group of MPs, which had been a protest group, now found itself more centrally placed in a party moving leftward. Its number swelled from forty-six to sixty-eight, then to eighty, in the two elections of 1974. This may have reflected a new kind of person wishing to become Labour MP; probably it represented the growing mood in the constituencies in favour of selecting a larger crop of like-minded candidates of the Left.

By 1974, the NEC which a decade before had been dominated by the Right (twenty to eight) was now in the hands of the Left, even though its superiority was slight, at fifteen to fourteen. The Women's Section and the Trade Union Section showed the main swing. This trend was to continue till in 1978 the Left was overwhelmingly in control.

Gulliver Stirs

The trade unions, whose earlier record had been of conservatism and bread-and-butter attitudes, were the key to the changes. They were numerically the most significant element of the Party Conference, accounting for 90% of Conference voting strength. When, therefore, they stirred in Conference, it was like Gulliver shifting his position. With their new-found militancy, aroused by their victory in the face of 'In Place of Strife', with leaders like Scanlon of the Engineers, and Jack Jones wielding a formidable one million TGWU votes, or a sixth of the Conference total, and Alan Fisher leading a left-wing NUPE which had recently tripled its numbers to 400,000, their influence was decisive.

The extreme left wing moved in with some success too. The Communists, who in the fifties and the sixties had either been proscribed by individual trade unions, or had rarely been found in the top echelons, were by the early seventies generally accepted by most unions and by the TUC and to be found at all levels of the movement. If the Communists suffered at this stage it was mainly through competition with other extreme left-wing bodies, some of whom had a greater appeal to the young. The International Socialists (IS) were successful in some of the white-collar unions. IS members won election to the executives of NALGO, ASTMS, APEX and other unions. The Workers' Revolutionary Party, the Socialist Labour League, a Trotskyite organisation, the International Marxist Group, the Maoist Communist Party of Great Britain, all with small memberships, could boast some success in penetration of the Party and in obtaining key union positions.

Although the Parliamentary Labour Party was still predominantly of the Right, it was now operating in a totally different climate. Within the walls of the Palace of Westminster, MPs could proceed much as before, but once outside Westminster it was another matter.

It is of course the function of Her Majesty's Opposition to oppose the Government of the day but both sides of the House may agree on certain issues. On Northern Ireland and on Rhodesia, Labour and Conservatives pursued identical policies. On domestic policies, however, Labour's attitudes in the House were very much the product of the party's own problems. Opposition to the Conservatives' incomes policies and trade union legislation stemmed more from Labour's need to rebuild bridges to the trade unions than from the intrinsic wrongness of the proposed Tory actions. For Wilson's

Government had itself pursued those same policies, curbing trade union power and introducing a statutory incomes policy.

As with the Common Market, so with domestic policies, Labour in opposition had executed a complete about-turn. The party was opposing for the good of the party and for the benefit of the unions. Even on the EEC question, the party was following the unions' new anti-EEC stand. At this stage, adversary politics fell into disrepute and, according to opinion polls, the public image of politicians took a knock. Particularly the close link with the unions was regarded with greater and greater misgivings by the general public. The unions were increasingly giving the impression of being a mighty institution outside the law, whose members could do as they wished on picket lines, and whose leadership could dictate terms to democratically elected governments. Two out of three people polled in 1972 thought the trade unions had more power than the Government. Finally, when Heath called an election following an extraordinary confrontation with the miners, on a 'Who governs Britain?' campaign, the answer seemed clear. In spite of three months' dispute, the three-day working week, and a state of emergency, or perhaps because of these, Heath lost the election. Not for nothing had the trade unions acquired their image. They had contributed to the Wilson Government's defeat in 1970. In 1974 they were undoubtedly the major factor in bringing down the Conservative Government. Their hat-trick was to be completed with Callaghan's downfall in 1979.

It had been a long decade since Wilson had given notice to the unions that Luddite attitudes had no place in the new society. If their militancy could have been harnessed for the benefit of society at large, they would not have acquired their labels of Robber Barons and Fourth Estate. In 1972, the year preceding the miners' strike, characterised by violence on the picket lines, the number of days lost through strikes reached a record 23.9 million. The Conservative Government's legislation to set certain legal restraints on union activities did reach the statute book but the Industrial Relations Act was a spur to greater militancy. And opposition to the Act had no greater champion than the Labour Party, for it promised to repeal the Act. In Parliament Labour MPs had slowed down the passage of the Bill during 450 hours of debate over a period of sixty days. Taverne recalls: "At report stage, we voted against every new clause and amendment proposed by the Government ... We even voted against amendments which were made at Labour's request." In 1974 Labour duly repealed the Act. The Labour Party had built bridges to the unions while in opposition. In government, after 1974, the work continued. In the words of Reg Prentice, a former cabinet minister of that era, the Labour Cabinet's method was simply: "Find out what the TUC wants and tell them they can have it."

Action Replay

Victory in 1974 should have heralded a new age of the Left. The Left of the Labour Party had been making the running during the three and a half years in opposition. The approach of the Labour Right in Government had been found wanting, and Labour had now won the election on a radical manifesto promising extensive nationalisation, an expansion of welfare provisions and a wealth tax; the quarrel with the unions had been patched up and a "compact" made to ensure closest co-operation between Government and the TUC.

But the administration from 1974 to 1979 turned out to be a re-play of 1964 to 1970. Wilson's Government had hardly taken office before it was again blown off economic course. Whatever its intentions, it failed to live up to the Left's expectations. Even had it wanted to, it could not afford to fulfil them.

The Right within the Party was no happier as pressures from the Left increased. The Left had by this time won control of the machinery of the Party and its objective was to tie Government and parliamentarians to the Party's wishes, both by changing the constitution of the Party, and through pressures on individual MPs.

Wilson's aim was to reconcile the increasingly irreconcilable. For much of the time, however, a pretence was kept up for the benefit of the outside world, that the growing split was a media invention.

Wilson started by balancing the two wings in Cabinet, notably with the addition of Michael Foot. Foot, the arch rebel of the Left, who had adorned every progressive platform and march in living memory, through a parliamentary career spanning almost four decades, biographer of Aneurin Bevan, former editor of the *Evening Standard* and *Tribune*, splendid old-style orator who, it was supposed, would live out his days as a back-bencher, was now called. Foot became Secretary of State for Employment. No-one would have guessed that this was the beginning of a new career which would culminate in the very highest position in the party.

Wilson's move was shrewd, for Foot was one of the heroes of the Left, liked even by those who did not share his views and, most important, trusted by the trade unions. His first act was to end the protracted miners' dispute by agreeing to support the NCB paying them a 29% increase, only 2% less than demanded. The country returned to a five-day working week. The state of emergency ended.

Compulsory wage restraint was also ended. The era of the Social Contract had begun, based on a gentleman's agreement rather than legal enforcement, allowing the unions their traditional role of wage bargaining but within a framework of voluntary and responsible partnership.

In return the Government was to repeal the much-resented Industrial Relations Act and its offspring the Industrial Relations Court, would provide food subsidies, freeze rents and introduce other socialist measures. But the trade-off failed. In the event the TUC was unable to deliver, for the unions would not be kept on the leash. Wage demands grew ever more steeply.

This was set against the background of a beleaguered economy. As in 1964 to 1970, difficulties were aggravated by the trade unions' reactions to national economic problems. A series of strikes, in the motor industry, on the railways, in hospitals, even before the election expected in the autumn (the second that year), augured badly for the future.

There were new international problems for Britain, as for every other country. In the autumn the price of oil had quadrupled, signalling the end of cheap oil. The economies of the world were about to suffer the protracted diseases of inflation and recession. Nowhere in the industrial world was the problem going to be more acute than in Great Britain.

Inflation had been surging ahead even before the oil crisis. Under the Conservatives it had already risen to around 10%. But this was nothing to what was to come. By 12 August 1975 inflation reached a record annual rate of 26.9% per annum. Up to the middle of 1974 the chief contributing factor had been high import costs. After this date wages took over as the principal cause.

While the Prime Minister continued to assure the country that the Social Contract was alive and well, wage claims were rising to unprecedented heights: 20%, 30%, even 80%. In the year up to June 1975, earnings for manual workers actually rose by 33.3% on average.

It was at this stage, in July 1975, that the voluntary

restraint policy of the Social Contract was superseded by a 'voluntary compulsory' pay policy. Jack Jones in the trade union movement and Foot in the Labour government steered the policy, ensuring its acceptance by the unions. Wage increases were to be restricted to £6 a week. At the same time, the Chancellor, Denis Healey introduced another "rough and tough" budget, with food and housing subsidies cut, a 2p increase in income tax, a rise to 25% in the VAT tax on so-called luxury items like washing machines, a rise in the car licence tax from £25 to £40 - all in addition to the traditional attack on the goose's golden eggs: tobacco, beer, spirits and wine. In spite of some favourable news, such as the raising of the threshold for income tax liability, this was a budget in the toughest tradition of Jenkins' 'hard slog' variety of the late sixties.

Bringing down inflation after the failure of the Social Contract policy brought its own problems, for deflation and lower wages led to a sharp rise in unemployment. Callaghan's inheritance on taking over as Prime Minister in the spring of 1976 was a tough one.

The postscript to the Wilson years was bitter for the Left. The toughest monetary policy yet seen was pursued by Callaghan and Healey to bring inflation down to single figures. And while in this they were successful, unemployment shot up to a new post-war record of 1,635,800. Foreign markets were still not convinced that public expenditure was sufficiently under control, in spite of Labour's successive stringent measures, and there was a dramatic slide in the pound. Healey was forced to borrow $3.9 million from the International Monetary Fund on terms dictated by the IMF through their representatives sent to London 'to check the books'; a further £3,000 million cut in public funding would have to be saved over the following two years.

In the face of such national economic difficulties the trade unions were at first co-operative. When the policy of the £6 maximum increase ended, they accepted two consecutive stages of tough restrictions, first of 4% increase per annum, later of 10%. When, however, against the advice of the TUC, Healey and Callaghan insisted on continuing with yet another round of 5% maximum per annum, the unions rebelled. The series of strikes which followed provided future history books with the phrase 'Winter of Discontent'.

These strikes effectively brought the Government down, in an election which Callaghan had, against all expectations, delayed till after the winter. Both the delay and the orthodoxy of the Government's policies came under attack from the Left, who saw these, rather than the strikes themselves, as the cause of electoral defeat.

The Left was bitter. The hard-won compact with the trade unions had been needlessly thrown away. Monetarist policies worthy of an orthodox Conservative government had been pursued, and socialism had not been advanced. Crisis after crisis had been stemmed by fingers-in-the-dyke policies; *ad hoc* measures had countered deep-seated problems. The vision proclaimed by Benn in opposition that "the crisis that we inherit when we come to power will be the occasion for fundamental change and not the excuse for postponing it", had proved a chimera.

But for this government survival itself had been a problem. It had either had only a tiny majority or, in a fragmented parliament, been in a minority. Callaghan's government had briefly even joined in a loose pact with the Liberals.

Despite these circumstances, reforms had been achieved. Legislation had outlawed discrimination on grounds of sex or race. The Employment Protection Act had given workers greater rights. The Education Act of 1976 had pushed on with universal comprehensive secondary education. Tenants had been given greater protection in law. The ship-building industry had been nationalised and the National Enterprise Board created. If the NEB was not quite the radical body intended in the Labour Programme of 1973, it was nevertheless, judging by the Tory outcry, a move in the direction of socialism.

If the Left was disillusioned, the Right was unhappy also. Disillusion had become a national phenomenon. Against a background of economic problems which successive governments of both major parties had been unable to solve, and with living standards under constant pressure, the whole country seemed to be in the grip of frustration.

The Conservatives, too, had problems. In 1975 they turned on their leader Edward Heath, whom they blamed for his government's failures, in contrast to the successes achieved by earlier post-war Conservative governments. Their solution was to look to the Right of their party by electing as leader the first woman to lead either party, Margaret Thatcher.

If evidence was needed of the general frustration during

this period, one had but to open any newspaper: the masochistic national pastime of self-criticism and the destructive lack of confidence in the British way of conducting the nation's affairs leapt from every page.

To foreigners, Britain's apparently suicidal behaviour was incomprehensible, and as more British travelled to the Continent as tourists or businessmen, it became obvious that the standard of living of a Hamburg docker or a Paris shopkeeper was now higher than the equivalent in Liverpool and London. This new reality was difficult to accept.

For the moderates within the Labour Party the pressures were even greater. The failures of the Party in government were their failures too. The view may have differed from those of the Left but rampant inflation and record levels of unemployment were clear evidence of failure for the whole party, Right or Left.

In politics, Labour moderates found themselves locked in a movement with people for whom they felt less sympathy than for many Liberals and even Conservatives. Roy Jenkins' description of the Labour Party as a coalation of incompatibles is no figure of speech.

What was more difficult to realise was that the natural order of things had changed, that the Labour Party was not the old Labour Party, and that the switch to the left was not merely an aberration of a few years, a kind of bad dream to be woken from, but that the change was more fundamental. It is true that many social democrats during the seventies, and some in the late sixties already, left the Party, but the majority stayed, believing it would all come right in the end.

In the words of one Social Democrat, one of the first to break out into the new party: "We were like the Jews in pre-war Germany. It was our country. Whatever was happening was bad and getting worse but it would be all right in the end. Some of us got out but late. Others stayed".

Those who did leave in the seventies left from frustration. Those who stayed played the game of unity and tried to pretend that things were not really so bad. Only twice were the rules of this game broken: the one time they fought was over the Common Market. The one time there was a genuine attempt at a break-out was Dick Taverne's trial run for Social Democracy.

Chapter Eleven

THE COMMON MARKET ISSUE

The Common Market and Britain's entry to it, has been the subject of heated political debate since its concept. It has also been used as a football in Labour Party tactics and thereby antagonised many followers.

In 1962, at the Brighton annual conference, Gaitskell had come down against British entry, voicing his doubts about "the end of 1,000 years of Britain's history". Although this had been a bitter blow for his social democrat supporters, paradoxically it had helped unite the movement after its convulsions over Clause 4 and unilateralism, as the Labour Party overall was sceptical about the EEC and not willing to be frog-marched in unquestioningly.

Nevertheless, the Labour Party made its position clear in the period 1964 to 1970 when Wilson was Prime Minister. Britain should go 'into Europe' if the terms were right. The words in which the Government's policy was expressed in those years suggested the view that entry was desirable *per se*. In a speech in 1966 Harold Wilson said: "Given a fair wind, we will negotiate our way into the Common Market, head held high, not crawl in." And indeed, although their efforts in 1967 were blocked by de Gaulle, these were real. Wilson and Brown made a whistle-stop tour of the capitals of the six EEC countries, and, having made their soundings, Wilson announced that full membership of the Community would be sought.

It was Wilson's vigorous advocacy of entry which converted many of the sceptics at this stage or at least ensured their acquiescence. He took with him a Cabinet which included a number of strong anti-Market ministers: Barbara Castle and Greenwood on the Left and Douglas Jay on the Right of the party; Benn in 1968 was more for than against. Wilson took the PLP with him, although many had previously been hostile. The NEC and Conference gave their approval. The House of Commons voted overwhelmingly for entry: 488 to 62.

Undoubtedly one of the important reasons for Wilson's and the Labour Government's decision to apply for entry was the economic situation at home. Europe provided a new initiative which could stimulate the economy and simultaneously serve as a distraction from the immediate harsh realities. That Labour's decision to apply in 1967 was not a temporary aberration was duly confirmed by the Labour Government's second application for membership, made after de Gaulle had retired.

When one month later in 1970,the Conservatives won the election, the Labour Party began to move back to its earlier scepticism. Wilson changed gear. His earlier whole-hearted support for entry changed to downright opposition or at best an ambiguous posture.

His aim was party unity, and as Wilson realised that the majority of the party was edging back to its earlier position against entry, he saw advantages in shifting the party position yet again. However, the difficulty was to balance all the pros and cons of changing position, to keep the party united, to derive the maximum benefit from opposing the Conservatives in their bid to achieve EEC membership, and ultimately to keep the option open for a future Labour government to join the EEC. But with this volte-face he began to lose the support of many Labour voters, who saw this as a lamentable display of opportunism and a corresponding lack of principles.

In Wilson's eyes, party unity came before the welfare of the country. His opposition to the Conservative government's bid for entry might well have been successful. A great triumph for the Party could have meant no entry into Europe, a policy direcly contrary to the one Wilson and his government had favoured while in office.

There were sound arguments for and against entry on both economic and political grounds. Voters could respect both, but the great drawback to opposing the very policy pursued while in office is that trust is shattered. Despite arguments and explanations, a reversal of policy was seen as both inconsistent and opportunistic, indicating tactics rather than principle. On domestic issues, Wilson also opposed the very policy he had pursued when in government. He had attempted to impose discipline on the trade unions, to introduce legislation modernising trade union practice. Now he fought the Conservative Government's attempt to do the same. Although Heath's Industrial Relations Act was not identical to Labour's proposals, the purpose was likewise to provide a legal framework for certain trade union practices, in particular for moderating strikes. As with the EEC issue, so with this, Labour's internal divisions impinged on party policy.

Wilson's "unity first" principle, though it had a certain effectiveness in the short-term, contained the seeds of party strife over the longer term. This was the moment when Labour's right wing found a natural standard bearer in Roy Jenkins. This was also the moment when the struggle for social democracy intensified. This was the time when realisation dawned on the Right that a formal split might become necessary; but, even in a Labour Party so divided, a popular issue was needed. The Common Market was not considered to be that issue. It was more likely to be a cause nearer home and unconnected with foreign policy, as proved to be the case in 1981.

However, in 1970 and 1971, the future was far from clear for the participants in the party drama. For the Right, with its back against the wall, the new turn of events was scarcely credible. At the annual conference in Autumn 1970, as an anti-market resolution was barely defeated, miners' leader Joe Gormley expressed the view: "I do not think it is good enough for us to say that we should change our policy on such important issues just because we do not happen to be in government."

By 1971 the anti-marketeers were winning the votes. The Government's White Paper detailing the proposed terms of entry was published in July 1971 and events followed swiftly that month. The Labour Party's diary began to fill up. On 17 July the Party held a special conference at the Central Hall, Westminster. Two days later, the PLP met to discuss Europe. Later that month, the NEC met. So did the TUC. The drift of the European debate was plain. The Party was coming down hard against entry on the terms gained.

At the special conference it is true that in the face of the passionate appeals against entry by Peter Shore and others, the pro-marketeers gave verbally as good as they got. Both qualitatively and quantitatively. They were given equal time by the conference chairman, Ian Mikardo, himself of the Labour Left and an avowed anti-marketeer. Winning the argument at the expense of a semblance of unity was not yet the overriding concern. For no vote was taken except a vote against the motion that a vote should be taken, defeated largely through Callaghan's efforts behind the scenes.

The NEC meeting came down sixteen to six against entry on present terms. The minority included Jenkins, Shirley Williams and Tom Bradley. The TUC leaders voted fifteeen to eleven against.

Wilson gave the lead in suggesting that the terms the Heath Government had achieved were less favourable than those that a Wilson government would have found acceptable. His attacks were often now tinged with opposition to the principle as well as the terms of entry.

But Wilson's and indeed the Party's position on the terms was more than a little undermined by the fact that the four Labour ex-ministers most intimately involved with the European question in Wilson's government now said they were happy with the terms set out in the Conservatives' White Paper. George Thomson, ex-Minister for Europe, said: "In my personal opinion these are terms which I would have recommended a Labour cabinet to accept." Lord Chalfont, his predecessor in the job, said he would vote in favour. George Brown, who as Deputy Leader and Foreign Secretary had with Wilson done the rounds of European capitals, said of the terms: "Challenging they may be, but they are fair." Michael Stewart, his successor as Foreign Secretary, said he would vote in favour of the terms. Could all these senior men involved in the original negotiations have got it wrong?

It was, however, Roy Jenkins who led the revolt on the day of the crucial vote. To the Parliamentary Labour Party, gathering two days after the special conference, he said: "I must express my own personal conviction that a Labour Cabinet would have accepted these terms by a large majority. That cannot be any more than an expression of a personal view. Others may take a different view. But I go a little beyond that. I believe that these terms are as good as those which those with any knowledge of the situation could realistically have hoped to get, certainly in 1967 with de Gaulle in power, and almost equally today. And I think that had we launched the application, and kept it in, and put behind it all the determination and enthusiasm which we did, without the intention of accepting the best terms which we could realistically expect, we would all of us have been guilty of wasting our own and a lot of other people's time as well."

The inconsistency of Wilson's position did not of course go unnoticed by the Government spokesmen either. Reginald Maudling, Home Secretary and Deputy Leader of the Conservatives, said of Wilson during a House of Commons

debate: "He reminds me of the young man of Brent
        Whose foot was unhappily bent
        To save himself trouble
        He bent it back double
        And instead of coming, he went."

The run-up to the historic debate in the House provided Labour with ample opportunity for heated and often bitter debate. At the beginning of October 1971, at the Labour Party conference, one resolution opposing entry on any terms was defeated by over a million votes. But the NEC resolution opposing entry on the terms of the White Paper and calling on all MPs to vote against the Government was carried overwhelmingly, five million to one million. Callaghan urged that "all members of the party should join hands on this issue and accept the verdict of the party."

The stage was set for the week-long 'final' debate in the House from 21 to 28 October 1971. As the parties went into the debate, that month's *Political Quarterly* attacked Wilson as a liability to the Labour movement: "Mr Wilson has proved himself unfit to be leader of the Labour Party."

On the day, while the Conservatives were free to vote according to their consciences, Labour imposed a three-line whip. As little heed was paid to this as to Callaghan's plea. Jenkins and sixty-eight Labour MPs voted with the Government; twenty Labour MPs abstained. Only the remaining two hundred "joined hands on this issue and accepted the verdict of the party." Had all Labour members voted against the Government, it would have been defeated and Edward Heath would have been unable to declare, that same day, 28 October 1971, that: "Parliament has now decided that Britain should, in principle, join the European Economic Communities on the basis of the arrangements which have been negotiated."

The following day, the *Guardian* reported: "Although there had been some early warning of the size of the Labour defection, the announcement of the Government majority (356:244) appalled Shadow Ministers." Labour loyalists saw this "as a catastrophe for the party, which had not been equalled since 1931."

In the House of Lords the vote gave the Government overwhelming support with 451 votes to 58. Thirty-eight Labour peers voted for entry, including many ministers in Wilson's government: the Lords George-Brown and Chalfont, the former Lord Chancellor, Lord Gardiner, Lord Diamond, a former Treasury Cabinet Minister and also junior ministers. Moreover Baroness Gaitskell, widow of the former leader who had expressed grave reservations about British entry into Europe, also voted in favour.

The *Guardian* reported that it was accepted by Shadow Ministers and back-benchers alike "that the knives would now be out for Labour rebels and that the repercussions would be felt in the party for years." Ten years later, Arthur Latham, one time chairman of the Tribune Group, wrote an article in *Tribune* headed 'How much tolerance should we tolerate?'. The article began: "Often when so-called moderates complain of intolerance they mean that we should agree with them. Certainly most Constituency Labour Parties were extraordinarily tolerant when sixty-nine Labour MPs let us down over the Common Market and then, by the most amazing chance, when always enough of them abstained or were absent so that Tory rebels just failed to defeat the Government on amendments to the EEC Bill." The article ended: "I am all for tolerance but my first principle is to defend those seeking to achieve socialist change, not those seeking to obstruct or betray it."

Although Roy Jenkins seriously considered resigning from the Party, he decided to soldier on. This was one of those moments when a break might have been possible, as the controversy continued, nurtured by the Bill's passage through the House. As Deputy Leader of the Labour Party, he was now at the peak of his career, with the highest reputation. It was an opportunity which, had Jenkins acted, might have changed the face of British politics, either by achieving social democracy ten years earlier or, as many thought more likely, by killing it prematurely.

Roy Jenkins did resign in April 1972 from the deputy leadership and from the Shadow Cabinet, though not from the Party. The deputy leadership he had only recently retained by fourteen votes in a contest against Michael Foot. The occasion of his resignation was the Party's support for an amendment calling for a referendum to approve Britain's entry, which, in the event, was defeated in the House, again with the help of Labour rebels, with sixty-three abstaining. Jenkins wrote to Wilson: "... the official majority position of the Party, which was only one of opposition to the terms of entry to the EEC, has increasingly become one of opposition in principle."

The Times, reporting Jenkins' resignation, wrote that it followed "the constant campaigning, high and low, to humiliate Labour's pro-marketeers''. Along with Jenkins, George Thomson and Harold Lever also resigned from the Shadow Cabinet. A few days later, Dick Taverne, David Owen and Dickson Mabon resigned their lesser ministerial posts. All three are now Social Democrats. Roy Hattersley, who was a fervent pro-marketeer, had been in that second wave of those intending to resign, but decided not to.

In July 1972 the Bill passed its third reading, and in January 1973 Great Britain was in Europe. But the story was by no means over. First, the Labour Opposition refused to co-operate by not sending its quota of Euro-MPs to the Strasbourg Parliament. Then, having become the party of government in 1974, Labour started up the whole tiresome process of "should we be in or out?" once again.

Wilson's Government re-negotiated certain aspects of the EEC arrangements. These re-negotiations were considered by observers as no more than useful. However, Wilson's new White Paper now stated that "continued membership of the Community is in Britain's interest." That position having been taken, another Labour Party special conference voted for the opposite: two to one for withdrawal. Terms having been re-negotiated, the people would now be invited to vote in a referendum on whether Britain should stay in or not.

It was decided that there would be yet another Great Debate in the country. Labour and Conservative politicians were free to engage in it according to their consciences. Strange alliances were temporarily formed. For example, Michael Foot and Enoch Powell were united against British entry, Roy Jenkins and Edward Heath for it. Finally, after months of Great Debate, the referendum produced a result of two to one for staying in.

In the end, what was it all about? The debate merely confirmed the status quo. It had been staged in the interests of maintaining Labour Party unity. At what a cost? As politicians concentrated on a debate which should never have taken place, Britain was actually going through a desperate economic crisis. The months of the 'debate' leading up to the referendum in June 1975 were precisely those during which the Social Contract was breaking down, when wages were spiralling upward and inflation rising to its highest post-war annual rate of 26.9%. While all minds should have been concentrating on this priority, the country had half its mind on the debate. Or to quote Roy Jenkins' words spoken in 1971 in another context: the Labour Party was "... guilty of wasting

84

our own and a lot of other people's time as well." Yet this issue was to be raised again within a few years.

Chapter Twelve

FIRST ATTEMPT AT SOCIAL DEMOCRACY

It is sometimes said there is nothing so powerful as an idea which has found its time. Conversely, there is nothing so vulnerable as an idea before its time, or so it proved to be with Social Democracy in 1974. Yet, might it have been otherwise?

One of the consequences of the Common Market dispute inside the Labour Party was that one man made a break with the Party, won a by-election under the label 'Democratic Labour', and transformed his own battle into a mini-run for Social Democracy. In the February 1974 General Election, Dick Taverne and four followers fought their premature Campaign for Social Democracy.

A fortnight before that election, *The Times* carried a leader under the heading 'Some do fight, fight and fight again', harking back to Hugh Gaitskell and an era of purposeful struggle. "The principles for which Mr Taverne and his little party are fighting are the principles of a responsible Labour party which Hugh Gaitskell fought for at Scarborough; they are the principles which have been too often allowed to fall by default in the Labour Opposition since 1970, or have been too coldly and weakly espoused."

Dick Taverne's endeavour was a heroic failure. Having failed to get backing from the heavy guns on the Right of his party, he decided to lead his own mini-charge. Inspiring it was, but on a scale quite inadequate to make any impact on the national scene.

Taverne was one of the sixty-nine MPs who voted for entry into the Common Market, against the three-line whip imposed by Wilson. Unlike the other sixty-eight Labour rebels, Taverne's action led him into a total rift with his constituency party. He had always been at odds with the local activists. This was connected with his previous relations with his own party in Lincoln, described in his book *The Future of the Left*. He had also had enough of national Labour politics based on opportunism and wanted to fight on a principle in which he believed passionately, the Common Market.

Taverne wrote: "Sometimes in the past one major issue has so deeply divided a party as to cause it to split; the Corn Laws led to the Peelite revolt from the Tories, and Irish Home Rule led to the secession of Chamberlain from the Liberals."*

He saw the Common Market issue in those terms - as a fundamental point where a clear stand had to be taken, but he was unable to take like-minded politicians with him. In the event, the EEC issue was not to be Labour's Corn Laws or Irish Home Rule.

Taverne had tried very hard to sell Jenkins the idea that this was the critical issue on which to fight. He tried to convince Jenkins of the argument that if he, Jenkins resigned, the Labour Party would split and the EEC Bill could be fought for by the breakaway party as a separate pro-Europe Labour Party. When Jenkins replied that "You, Dick and I might want to see a new party, but there is no general support", that killed an early opportunity. The Jenkinsites went on to fight for the EEC Bill from inside the Labour Party. On 28 October 1971, Jenkins, Taverne and sixty-seven others voted for entry with the Conservatives.

Within less than three weeks, on 16 November 1971, Taverne was facing a motion of 'No Confidence' in his Lincoln constituency. It was carried, but only just, by fifty-five to fifty-one. The fact that this was the only time that Taverne had voted against a three-line whip, whereas Michael Foot and other leading Tribunites had done so regularly, did not help Taverne's case. Taverne also points out in his defence that the local party had been happy enough to campaign against Conference decisions ten years earlier when it backed unilateralism while the Party had swung against. The EEC issue may have been a point of genuine disagreement but its use as a weapon against Taverne was a feature of the power struggle between two wings of the Party, a microcosm of the power struggle in the Party nationally.

In the meantime, Taverne was promoted by Wilson to be the official economic spokesman, second to Roy Jenkins, showing that the "Parliamentary Party and even the Leader of the Party took a different view of my act of rebellion from my local party." But the local dispute rumbled on with the activist Left gunning for their MP. They had another chance in April,

---

* From *The Future of the Left* by Dick Taverne, Jonathan Cape, 1974

when Taverne resigned as Shadow Minister in the wake of the resignations of Jenkins, Thomson and Lever.

The vote on 16 June 1972 went seventy-five to fifty against Taverne. The result had not been in doubt but Taverne had taken the opportunity to arrange for a local poll to ascertain the broader view in the constituency. The results, a few days before the crucial vote, had shown overwhelmingly that the electorate approved his actions. Of over six hundred people questioned, the support was three to one for Taverne's right to vote in accordance with his views rather than with the Party. They approved eight to one of Taverne as their Member of Parliament. In a subsequent poll, carried out by the Opinion Research Centre in October 1972, this was confirmed with 82% in favour of Taverne and only 2% who thought he was a bad MP.

Taverne lodged an appeal. The NEC became the final arbitrator, as was proper within the rules of the Party. What was more questionable was the subsequent sequence of decisions. The NEC's Committee of Inquiry found there had been a breach of natural justice and a failure to consult ordinary Party members. They recommended unanimously that Taverne's appeal should be upheld. The next higher echelon, the Organisation Sub-Committee, accepted the recommendation, but only on its chairman's casting vote. The next day the NEC voted twelve to eight against Taverne, dismissing his appeal, for, in Taverne's words, "As the left wing had a majority in the NEC there could be no possible chance of winning." That was in July.

In October, during the Party conference, Taverne resigned dramatically. He would have liked to go into battle as part of a new social democratic movement. As it was, in March 1973 he fought alone in a solitary by-election in Lincoln. While it created a great deal of interest and while many on the Right of the Labour Party secretly wished him well, they were not ready to risk their careers by backing him. Indeed, they would have preferred him not to expose himself or the Labour Right at all. Nor did the Right wish to lose Taverne from inside the Party. Years later many were repeating how they had tried to dissuade him from making the break. Taverne, one of 'Gaitskell's blue-eyed boys', was always considered one of the brightest of his generation, who would go far. The *Financial Times* wrote before the break was final (4 August 1972): "A party which will not even try to accommodate him and a leader who dare not lift a finger to help him is indeed in a mess."

After his resignation Taverne kept himself to himself, not seeing his Labour colleagues. Two months were to elapse before he saw Jenkins again, in December 1972. With their wives over dinner, they talked. Taverne tried again to persuade Jenkins as he had sought to do before. He was convinced he would win the by-election. Says Taverne now: "I suggested to Jenkins that he should speak up for me. That my victory would be his victory. He could come over straightaway with a dozen or so MPs. He could become Prime Minister at the first go. To which Jenkins said: 'Yes, lots of people tell me that but they may not be representative of the electorate.' "

So Taverne went on alone. But in Lincoln he was not alone. There, tremendous enthusiasm permeated his campaign. Volunteers flooded in from all over the country. One journalist likened the atmosphere to the spirit which fired Senator Eugene McCarthy's presidential campaign in 1968. The by-election was a great victory for Taverne. For in spite of Labour pouring a hundred MPs and countless of its supporters into the area, Taverne, as an independent Democratic Labour candidate, was re-elected MP on an extraordinary 58.2% of the vote. The Labour candidate polled 23% and the Conservative 18%.

It was on the strength of that truly staggering victory that Taverne decided to widen the campaign. First he fought the local elections and took over Lincoln town hall with the Tavernites winning a large majority. He then went national. Unfortunately, the timing proved disastrous. For in the midst of the miners' strike, with the fear that Heath would call an election and wishing to be ready for this, Taverne played his hand. He would contest a number of seats for Social Democracy with a team of four. This was in the middle of January. The election was held on 28 February. Six weeks preparation was not enough.

Taverne was again returned but with a much reduced majority. His associates were routed, each polling under a thousand votes: James Robertson fought Anthony Wedgwood Benn in Bristol South East while John Martin fought left-winger Norman Atkinson in Tottenham. Voters had had no time to learn about the new type of Labour candidate. The concept meant nothing to them. They voted for traditional Labour and the Social Democrats vanished without a trace. In the October elections, even Taverne was beaten - by a few hundred votes. That was the end of the experiment, though Social Democrats remained in Lincoln town hall to the time of the Limehouse Declaration and beyond.

The Times wrote then about the 1974 Social Democrats: "Some of them may win few votes, but the idea for which they stand is certainly a significant one." Wedgwood Benn talked about a creation of the media. In 1981, he and his colleagues on the Labour Left were to continue to talk of Social Democrats in the same terms. In 1972/3 Taverne's parliamentary friends for the most part thought he would not even win the first by-election. Bob Maclennan, himself in 1981 in the first wave of Social Democrats, then predicted that the Labour Party would never split.

Had Labour lost the election of 1974, events might have developed differently. A re-gouping of Right and Left might have followed Labour's defeat, or so went Taverne's own projected scenario. He now says: "My venture in Lincoln had little hope of attracting a wider public. I intended to show the flag and wait till Labour either lost the elections or was defeated by the Social Contract. But Labour won and Jack Jones saved the Party. I was happy to go. There was not much point or fun going on alone."

Yet Taverne did not have to be alone. A poll commissioned by *The Times* in September 1972 showed that a larger proportion of the electorate would support a new grouping of the centre than would support either Conservative or Labour. Taverne spoke of twelve million Jenkinsites. Less than a decade later the fantasy had become reality. Jenkins, departing for his President's job in Brussels, is reported to have said then in 1976 that the greatest mistake of his political life was not to have supported Dick Taverne in Lincoln.

Chapter Thirteen

THE FRUSTRATED SOCIETY

Within the British electorate an ever-growing number of people were unhappy with the political scene. Democracy was not functioning as it should. While Britain might be renowned as the country of democracy and tolerance and of parliamentary tradition, many within this political utopia were feeling disenchanted, not to say disenfranchised. For what use democracy when in effect it means voting for one of two possible governments, either Conservative or Labour, and when neither is the voter's real choice?

From the mid-sixties, Britain was blown off course. There was a feeling in the air that the country was drifting from crisis to crisis with no-one adequately in control. Why was Britain in decline? Why should the country which had won the war and 'saved the world' be doing worse than its neighbours and, above all, than Germany, the defeated enemy? Why should Britain, which had controlled a quarter of the world, now be reduced to the level of a second-ranking country? Why was Britain running down? And whilst the country was doing badly, politicians were merely squabbling and blaming one another. The electorate stood powerless on the sidelines. One of the main reasons why it was impotent was that the basis upon which British politics were run gave it no power to change the status quo. With the constituency system based on winner-takes-all, with non-winning votes going totally to waste, there seemed no chance of a break-through by a third party, whether Liberal or any other.

A party could gain a quarter of the votes of the country and still only finish up with a handful of seats in the House of Commons. So while polls could indicate that millions of people would prefer a new political party of the centre, usually seen in terms of some re-grouping of the Labour Right and the Liberals, there was no way of transforming this desire into positive winning votes at the polling booths. The new political grouping was a mirage in the British political desert, because

91

the Labour Right and the Liberals did not exist as one political party.

The Liberals on their own, and we shall look at their progress in a moment, did not have a winning, government-forming formula; to vote Liberal was seen as wasting a vote. The Labour Right would not sever its links with the Labour movement, for the electoral system made this too much of a leap into the unknown, too much of a gamble for careful politicians. So the Labour Right-Liberal link was to remain untested till the internal pressures within the Labour Party became far greater, and till the electorate had prepared the ground with ever clearer signals that such a group could succeed. This took a good decade longer than many, fervently wishing for a change, would have liked.

In the meantime, the electorate's signals of protest came in many forms. Many people stopped voting. In 1950 and 1951 over 80% of the electorate voted. At subsequent general elections the percentage dropped. Fewer people voted in 1970 than in 1950, although the electorate had increased by six million people, with eighteen-year-olds entitled to vote for the first time: in 1970 28.3 million voted, as against 28.7 million in 1950 - 72% against 84% of the electorate.

And fewer of the dwindling number of voters chose major parties. In 1951 97% of the votes went to Labour or the Conservatives. In the two 1974 elections, the two parties attracted only 75% of the vote. Seen another way, in 1951, four out of five people turned out to vote Labour or Conservative; in 1974 only three out of five; and by 1981 opinion polls indicated that a mere two out of five would vote Labour or Tory, because by this time a genuine alternative had become available, namely the SDP/Liberal Alliance.

Just how unenthusiastic the electorate was about the two parties can be seen clearly from the table below. This shows the percentage of the electorate voting Conservative and Labour during each election since 1951. For Labour the pattern is down all the way with, the single exception of the 1966 election interrupting the decline. Where in 1951 over 40% of the electorate voted Labour, by October 1974, and again in 1979, only 28% turned out to do so.

The Conservatives' vote also declined from 1951 to October 1974, from 39.6% to just over 26%, an even greater loss of support than in Labour's case. Later, in the 1979 victory, the Tories halted the decline with an impressive upturn, though in the light of the Thatcher administration's unpopularity, this too is likely to be only a respite in the overall decline.

	% of Electorate Casting Votes for Labour	% of Electorate Casting Votes for Conservatives
1951	40.26	39.6
1955	35.59	38.12
1959	34.51	38.93
1964	34.00	33.46
1966	36.31	31.76
1970	30.96	33.41
1974 (Feb)	29.20	29.83
1974 (Oct)	28.54	26.06
1979	28.04	33.36

The electorate in the meantime was switching votes to the Liberals. Though this could not swell the number of Liberal MPs in the House, voters were making their views plain: the trend showed up particularly clearly following Conservative administrations, for voters were increasingly opposing the Tories by voting Liberal in preference to Labour, as seen below:

% of Votes Cast

	1959	1964	1974 (Feb)
Liberal	5.9	11.2	19.3
Conservative	49.4	43.4	37.9
Labour	43.8	44.1	37.1

An extraordinary rise in Liberal votes produced a handful of additional MPs.

Even so, voting outside of the traditional government parties was probably still largely protest voting. Arguably, parliamentary by-elections became the clearest indicators of how the electorate actually felt. Then votes were registered on equal terms between the parties, for to vote for either major or minor party would have no bearing on the government of the day, and people could afford the luxury of voting exactly as they felt. By-elections often showed extraordinarily large swings against the major parties, in particular against the party holding office at the time. Thus Labour enjoyed a series of by-election victories from 1962 to 1964, at the tail end of the Tories' long years in power, winning a string of seats from the Conservatives: Middlesbrough West, Glasgow Woodside, South Dorset, Bristol South East, Luton and Rutherglen.

However, from that moment on, the electorate's disenchantment with Labour was almost continuous. It is a remarkable fact that between 1964 and 1981, the Labour Party managed to win only one seat from the Conservatives and one from Independent Labour. These gains were in the period of the Heath government, when Labour won Bromsgrove from the Tories in 1971 and regained Merthyr Tydfil from Independent Labour in 1972.

During that same seventeen-year period, Labour lost many by-elections, and although the Party could console itself that a good proportion of seats lost were regained at general elections, even that consolation was, on closer inspection, unreal, since it ignored the fact that Labour's loss of support, nationwide, was continuous. Over a quarter disappeared in the post-war years.

Whatever success Labour had in regaining lost by-election seats, and indeed in winning general elections, the reality was stark: the electorate's enthusiasm for the Party was ebbing. Closer inspection of by-elections shows the dramatic, if at that stage impotent, protest against Labour. Each of the periods 1966-70, 1970-1974, and 1974-9 tells its own story.

From 1966 to 1969 there was an absolutely disastrous run of by-elections, with massive swings against Labour. No less than sixteen of Labour's parliamentary seats were lost, twelve to the Conservatives, one to the Liberals, one to the Scottish Nationalists and two to the Welsh Nationalists. The average swing against Labour in this period was 16.8%, although some of the individual defeats were far in excess of the average. For example, the loss of Birmingham Ladywood to the Liberals was on a swing of 30.6%. Hamilton, which they had not contested previously, was won by the Scottish Nationalists with 46%.

These swings away from Labour were happening against a background of economic crises: runs on the pound, devaluation, deflation, unemployment, troubles with unions and the feeling that the Government was not in control. The loss of seats to Welsh Nationalists, Scottish Nationalists and Liberals, though all regained in the subsequent 1970 general election, was an early warning of much worse to come: these three parties would be making unprecedented inroads into British politics at the 1974 general elections.

In the 1970-74 period of Conservative Government, Labour's by-election warning signals took another form. For this, if anything, should have been the mirror image of the previous administration: the Conservatives were in great trouble, unable to control either the economy or trade union relations. It was a period of growing inflation, unemployment reaching three-quarters of a million, unprecedented strikes and extreme trade union problems.

Labour should now have benefited from the Tories' discomfiture in exactly the way the Tories had done from Labour's administration of the late sixties. Not a bit of it. During the three and a half years in question, Labour succeeded in winning only Bromsgrove from the Conservatives. A truly poor tally in the circumstances. But the picture was worse than that. The Conservatives were actually losing seats, but not to Labour. It was the Liberals who were picking up the anti-Tory vote. In less than one year, between December 1972 and November 1973, the Liberals took four Conservative seats. They won Sutton & Cheam, and Berwick on Tweed, and even managed to win the Isle of Ely and Ripon on the same day.

To add insult to injury, Labour in opposition was losing seats. Apart from losing Lincoln to Dick Taverne, they also lost Rochdale to Liberal Cyril Smith and Glasgow Govan to the Scottish Nationalists.

In government again from 1974 to 1979, Labour lost six more seats to the Conservatives and one to the Liberals. The pattern of several administrations from the mid-sixties to the end of the seventies was consistent and was, from Labour's point of view, consistently bad. Perhaps it was most worrying that, when the major party of opposition should have been exploiting the government party's unpopularity, Labour was unable to capitalise on it.

Given this kind of historical background, the Croydon North West by-election in October 1981 provided precisely the result which should have been expected. When the Liberal Bill Pitt won on a Liberal/SDP Alliance ticket, he won on a swing of 29.5%. But the commentators were suggesting that, had it not been for the new Alliance, Labour should normally have won such a by-election. On the contrary, even without the new Alliance, Labour's record since the mid-sixties indicated defeat in Croydon North West.

The electorate was thus making repeated attempts over the years to emerge from its straightjacket. In 1974, the electorate nearly managed it, and the results were quite startling for British politics.

As the Leader of the Liberals, Jeremy Thorpe said a week after the elections: "Looking round the House, one realises that we are all minorities now - indeed, some more than others." For whilst Labour had won the election, it was in a minority against all other parties, which included Liberals, Scottish and Welsh Nationalists, Ulster Unionists, and independent MPs including Taverne. At the second election in 1974, Labour's position improved, but so did that of the Nationalist parties, though the Liberals slipped back a little. The Nationalists had made a tremendous advance which was to influence British politics in the next parliament, and with the rise of nationalism in Scotland and Wales, break-up of the United Kingdom had even become a possibility.

The 1974 elections were a vote of No Confidence in the major parties and in the system. The composition of the House bore no relation to people's wishes.

First, in February 1974, the electorate voted marginally in favour of the Tories: 37.9% as against 37.1% of the votes. Second, both major parties represented minorities, as Thorpe had pointed out: with over a third of the votes cast, and over a quarter of the electorate casting their vote positively for Labour (28.5%). The result was a Labour government.

The Scottish and Welsh Nationalist parties which had previously won single seats only, mainly at by-elections, now swept in with fourteen seats between them, eleven for the Scots and three for the Welsh Nationalists. The Liberals marginally increased their representation in the House, and it was here that the gravest injustice was done, both to the Liberals and to the electorate. Over six million Liberal votes brought only fourteen parliamentary seats: with every fifth person voting Liberal, only every forty-fifth seat in the House became Liberal. A system of proportional representation would have resulted in 120 seats for the Liberal Party.

No measures for introducing any form of proportional representation were taken because the existing system favours the major parties. As long as the what-we-have-we-hold parties, as Jenkins called them, felt their turn would come, there was no incentive for change. Yet, opinion polls during the late seventies, in the aftermath of the anomalous 1974

96

elections, all consistently showed the public in favour of electoral reform, in a ratio of five to two, and even five to one, irrespective of party allegiance.

The electorate having nowhere else to go, merely turned to one of the two parties in ever diminishing numbers and twelve million Jenkinsites indicated to a *Times* opinion poll that they were waiting in the wings. However, they could not emerge. They would only do so in sufficient numbers when it became clear that they had power to vote for a potential party of government.

During the seventies, progressive people found different outlets for their energies and beliefs. Many, disillusioned by the infighting or the futility of the available progressive political party, went outside the Labour Party, often outside the sphere of parliamentary politics altogether.

Thus pressure movements promoting single issues sprang up or were given fresh impetus by people who had opted out of a Labour movement which they would earlier have regarded as a natural home. Many felt that radical reforms could more easily be achieved in this way. Others felt that concentration of their efforts on an important social issue was more valuable than participation in a reforming movement hindered by an atmosphere of bitter internal strife.

The public became increasingly aware now of the existence of pressure groups, of the problems they confronted and of the need for specific improvements in society. To name but a few of these: Child Poverty Action Group, MIND (previously known as the National Association for Mental Health), Shelter (which exists to provide homes for the homeless), Campaign for Homosexual Equality, Age Concern, The National Council for Civil Liberties, Gingerbread (which sets out to help one-parent families). Other movements existed to improve race relations, improve the lot of women, fight drugs, alcoholism and smoking, help prisoners and their families, help those with problem marriages or unwanted pregnancies. There were many other causes engaging the energies of progressive people.

The most important and worldwide movement was the Ecology Party which, as Germany's "Green" party, already has seats in some of the provincial 'Länder' parliaments. In Britain, at its first attempt in the 1979 election, it won a creditable 2% of the votes in the fifty-three constituencies the party contested. At about the same time there was a renaissance of the Campaign for Nuclear Disarmament which found much popular support here and abroad.

Unilateral nuclear disarmament became official Labour party policy where twenty years earlier, though it had aroused great passions within Labour, it had ultimately been rejected. If Labour in the late seventies chose an issue which had considerable appeal, the Party's overall appeal was dropping. The Labour Party, aware over many years that something was radically wrong, that people were moving away from the party, both as party workers and as voters, gave conflicting analyses and conflicting remedies to the sickness. The result was ever more bitter conflict.

Chapter Fourteen

THE DEMORALISED RIGHT: RELUCTANT FELLOW TRAVELLERS OF THE SEVENTIES

At the time of the February 1974 election, there were many Labour sympathisers who would have preferred the Party to be defeated rather than to win. They feared that victory would strengthen those tendencies within the party with which they could not identify: intolerance, undemocratic attitudes, and a drift to the left which ultimately would appeal to too small a part of the electorate and lead to the end of Labour as a serious political alternative. In their view, only from the ashes of a Labour defeat could a new, social-democratic style Labour Party with wide appeal arise.

In the event, Labour won the election on a minority vote lower than that of the Tories. Many of the Right's fears were to be realised. Victory strengthened the Left's hand. For the next five years under Wilson and Callaghan, whatever conservative policies may have been pursued by the Government, the Left attacked on all fronts within the Party. The Right never acted, never mounted a forceful campaign worthy of the name. There was inadequate will to win the battle for the soul of the party. The Right merely reacted. It was an ignominious time for the Right - merely hanging on. The Right could console itself with the belief that it held the levers of power. Was the Labour Party not traditionally a moderate body, primarily a partnership of pragmatic parliamentarians and trade unionists, and was the present tendency therefore not merely a temporary aberration? Was Labour not the party of government? The boat must not be rocked. Sooner or later all would be well. In the meantime, the Right would keep a low profile, be a moderating influence where it could, protest when exceptionally provoked, and wait. The problem was that the Right's tolerance to provocation grew with time, and the Left became bolder and more aggressive. And the Right, in the tradition of appeasers confronted by an opponent set on victory, misjudged its ability to appease successfully.

99

There were of course those of the Labour Right who said then: "this far and no further". But their words fell on barren ground. There was no Social Democratic Party to move to, no viable alternative. Right-wing dissidents could leave politics, move to the Liberals, like Christopher Mayhew, or in rare cases cross over to the Tories, like Reg Prentice. As Bernard Levin wrote in *The Times* (21 February 1974): "I do find myself staring into a mirror when I think of Thomas Mann's words: 'I am a man of balance. I instinctively lean to the left when the boat threatens to capsize on the right, and vice versa', and that, indeed, is why I have been compelled to move to the right in recent years, as the Labour Party boat has lurched further and further to the left and threatened to drown us all."

However, the instincts of moderate men inside the Party were quite different. Instead of leaning hard to the right, they shifted leftwards in the centre of the boat, thereby making their own contribution to the dangerous list to the left. This was the era of compromise, of fudging, the heyday of the Wilson style Labour Party.

The real problem confronting the Labour Party was the fact that the desperate plight of the working class, which had been responsible for its birth, was enormously improved. Pensions, unemployment and sickness benefits, and the whole welfare package had changed the life of the working man and made it relatively acceptable. The crusading fervour of the working-class voter was disappearing fast, and the politicians were, to some extent, forced to espouse causes and measures which, by singling out the working class, accentuated class distinctions.

Gaitskell in 1959 had tried to bring about a classless party, one which would be a party of nation rather than of class, a party which would represent all the people rather than the 'working people'. His failure to persuade the Party to become a modern Labour Party, and the failure of the Party to recognise the need for change, were the pre-conditions for the subsequent developments. Had the Labour Party been far-seeing enough to change course then in 1959, as did the German Socialist Party, the SPD, the Labour Party might well have become the natural party of government, not by default of the electoral system, but as of right, as the progressive party of the people as a whole.

However, Gaitskell failed. His successor, Wilson, failed to try. The result was a divided and, even more important, a divisive Labour Party, exacerbating rather than healing class differences in the country.

Yet the changes which were taking place in Britain were evident. As Conservative politician, R A Butler described it: "The class escalators are continually moving and people are divided not so much between 'haves' and 'have-nots' as between 'haves' and 'have-mores'". While there was scope for considerable improvements in society, the worst excesses had been eliminated, according both to Butler and to Labour right-wingers.

Shirley Williams has put it another way. In her book, *Politics is for People*, she wrote: "The welfare state and the publicly financed health services largely eliminated crude primary poverty". She also wrote: "The modern post-industrial economy is very different from nineteenth-century industrialism. A declining minority of the population is employed in factories, the birthplace of the industrial proletariat. More and more people are in white-collar and professional jobs. A traditional socialism steeped in old industrial attitudes and based on the class war has become obsolete."

Many politicians were preaching compassion and reforms for the whole of society rather than for the so-called working class alone. Particularly since the working class was moving up on Butler's 'escalator' and class distinctions were becoming blurred. Certainly the view expressed by Gaitskell in November 1959, shortly after Labour's election defeat, tied in with the Conservative politician's statement seven months later: "Again and again, I have heard the same story, of the relatively prosperous younger married couples who, having moved from older houses in solid Labour areas to new, attractive housing estates, lost their Labour loyalty and voted Conservative."

"In short, the changing character of labour, full employment, new housing and new life-styles based on the telly, the fridge, and the car, and the glossy magazines, all these have had their effect on our political strength." He also said on that same occasion: "Let us remember that we are a party of the future, not of the past ... It is no use waving the banners of a bygone age." One of his six principles of Socialism was "a belief in a classless society, without snobbery, privilege or restrictive social barriers."

Sociologist and Director of the London School of Economics, Ralf Dahrendorf wrote in *The Guardian* (19 July

1979): "No myth about Britain seems harder to dispel than that concerning class. ... Take the loose meaning of class for social strata, distinguished from others by income and status. ... By comparison to other OECD countries, income differentials in Britain are near the average, the basic status of citizens is if anything higher in relative terms, social mobility, notably through education, has long been pronounced (certainly more pronounced than in Germany). I would suggest that there is not one index of social stratification by which Britain differs significantly from other developed countries. ... It is no more a class society than any other advanced society in the OECD world."

Social mobility was also the theme of the *New Stateman's* political editor, Peter Kellner (30 October 1981): "... the sense of class solidarity which propelled Labour to power in 1945 has all but evaporated. Even as late as 1964, 50% of the electorate said they thought of themselves as 'belonging to a particular social class', and most of these - 34% of the whole electorate - considered themselves working class.* This summer (1981) MORI asked a national sample of voters an identical question. Despite the recession, which might have been expected to increase class consciousness, only 29% said they belonged to a particular class, and barely half - 15% of the total sample - said working class .... For anyone seeking to understand why Labour's support has been leaking away for thirty years, that is possibly the most telling fact of all." Labour had been fighting the wrong war all this time: a class war instead of a war for society as a whole, a war which harped on divisions between people which are no longer valid, and which itself exacerbated divisions. *

When Denis Healey talked of squeezing the rich till the pips squeaked, he was speaking the language of the Labour Party competing in extravagance with the voices on the Left of his party. 'The politics of envy' was a phrase that gained currency to describe the new mood. Labour, which had been seen as occupying the moral ground of politics, came to be seen as the party of intolerance and division.

Perhaps, there was an in-built fear that to do away with class distinction would lose Labour its *raison d'etre*. Indeed, there is a tradition evident in one section of the Labour movement, the trade unions, which would seem to confirm a

* From *Political Change in Britain* by Butler and Stokes, Macmillan, 1969

preference for 'them and us' rather than 'all of us together'. Trade unions have an innate suspicion of working too closely with management: worker directorships, for example, are thought by many trade unionists to blur a proper distinction. Co-operation Scandinavian or American style between unions and management is still seen as a less than desirable substitute for a straight confrontation between adversaries. 'Them and us' provides a clear demarcation between traditional opponents, preferable to the danger of being compromised by the 'agents of capitalism'.

Yet unions co-operating with managements in the USA, Scandinavia, Germany and elsewhere have earned a higher standard of living for their members than have British trade unions. Co-operation, emphasis on what unites rather than what divides, has achieved considerably more.

The great philosophical division inside the Labour Party has regrettably been between those who wished to pursue politics for the whole of society, and those who pushed class interests even when the working classes no longer saw themselves as such. Labour's adopted aim, to bring about an irreversible shift in the balance of power and wealth in favour of working people and their families, was as out of date as it was dogmatic and divisive. It gave a spurious unity to Labour's programme but not broad electoral appeal.

In Kellner's words, Labour's support had been leaking away for thirty years. Nor was new blood flowing in, according to Graham Hough in his essay 'Freedom in Danger': "Mass migrations are not common in British politics and individual changes of opinion may have no more than individual significance. But if the individual changes are all in the same direction it seems to suggest something. Has anyone actually joined the Labour Party in the last few years? If so, no one has heard of it."*

The active membership of the Party had been sliding for a long time, causing concern to the leadership. The post-war heyday of one million members had dropped to two-thirds that of figure by the mid-seventies. Yet even that is misleading. To quote Ron Hayward, then General Secretary,they are 'fictitious membership figures'.

In the fifties, when membership reached its highest levels, the figures were generally supposed to be correct. Constituency Labour parties were affiliated to the national

---

* In *Right Turn*, edited by Patrick Cormack, published by Leo Cooper, 1978

Labour Party, with affiliation fees based on a minimum 240 members. When in 1962 this was changed to a minimum 1,000 members, CLPs had little option but to send their money, regardless of whether they had reached that number or not. The membership of the Party by the mid-seventies was more likely around 300,000, a very substantial decline from the post-war million, but the estimate is in line with the Houghton Committee Report on Party Finance (1976) which calculated constituency Labour parties' average membership at only five hundred. Yet even that is an exaggeration because the number of members in a CLP who actually do the work, attend meetings - the so-called activists - is estimated at between fifty and one hundred.

It was precisely because the local unit was so small that those determined enough could take it over. This has caused much controversy as well as difficulty for the social democrats within the Labour parties, for it was not they who were creating the pressures to take control of CLPs but the Left - and a Left of many hues. Broadly speaking, it could be divided into a democratic and an extremist, undemocratic Left, prepared to use democratic machinery for an ultimately undemocratic objective.

The undemocratic Left had become increasingly active since the end of proscription in 1973, which allowed the emergence of 'parties within the party' in groups, often highly organised and dedicated to their task of infiltration. A new word became fashionable to describe their relationship with the Labour Party - entryism. Trotskyites, Maoists, and the Militant Tendency were making inroads into the Labour Party. Since the electoral system in the country gave these groups no realistic chance of winning seats in their own name, their way to political influence had to be through the Labour Party and through the trade unions, in both of which they had considerable success.

Yet the Labour Party had, to say the least, an ambiguous relationship with the non-democratic Left. 'No witch-hunt' was the underlying attitude. Yet, from time to time, when the activities of the extreme Left could no longer be ignored, Labour voices were raised, although they mostly scoffed at the idea of any real threat: 'Reds under the beds' was just Tory politicking.

Nevertheless, Callaghan as Prime Minister did speak out: "There are too many of these people who have infiltrated this party already. Get them out." Harold Wilson referred to "an unrepresentative caucus" and to "the calculated actions of what we in Yorkshire call 'comers-in'." Shirley Williams, four years before the Limehouse Declaration, was much concerned with the problem of the 'comers-in'. In a speech on 22 January 1977 in Derbyshire, devoted entirely to Labour democracy under threat and to extremist socialist doctrines creating that threat, she spoke of " 'Trotskyism' - that mysterious political doctrine which we hear so much about but which few of us really know" and of "modern Trotskyism, like the Troskyism of Trotsky himself" which "holds liberty and democracy in total contempt." She spoke of the necessity of acting only with the consent of the people, with the implication that not everyone inside the Labour Party thought this way: "Consent is sometimes talked about - including by many Marxists - as though it were a luxury, a sort of optional extra, something that is nice to have but is not absolutely necessary. I disagree ... In any case, what is the opposite of consent? It is, of course, compulsion."

The Labour Party should not welcome all and she concluded: "We are entitled to ask of those who wish to join us: 'Do you share our belief that our socialist objectives must be achieved by the method of democracy? Do you share our belief in the liberty of each individual human being, in his or her right to express his opinions and religious beliefs truly and without fear of the consequences? Are you prepared to say, so long as the system of parliamentary democracy is maintained in this country, that you will rule out violence as means to the achievement of your political ends? Do you accept that, if the cause of socialism (as you define it) and the cause of democracy should come into conflict, you will stand by democracy?'

"We are entitled to ask these questions. We are entitled to unequivocal answers to them. In my view, someone who is not prepared to give an unequivocal, unhesitating 'Yes' to every one of these questions does not belong in the Labour Party at all."

The most notorious and successful Trotskyite, revolutionary group, the Militant Tendency, continued to be tolerated in 1981, though by then, under the pressure of Michael Foot who was concerned to stop the drift of right-wingers out of the Party, it was to be the subject of an investigation, following an earlier investigation, the results of which had been ignored.

By 1981, five Militants had been selected as

Parliamentary candidates. There are also six Militant councillors in Liverpool and a few elsewhere. No less than fifty to one hundred of the delegates to Conference from the 635 CLPs in 1981 were Militants. The Tendency's earliest success was the nomination of Labour Party Young Socialists, whose representative was a member of the National Executive Committee.

Another early leftist triumph came with the appointment of Andy Bevan as Labour's National Youth Officer. Bevan, no relation to Aneurin Bevan, was both a Labour Party Young Socialist and a Militant. His nomination required the approval of the NEC. Callaghan, the Prime Minister, contrary to his normal practice, decided to intervene and argued powerfully against the appointment. Tony Benn argued equally powerfully in favour of Bevan. He argued that Bevan's brand of Marxism harked back to the marxist heritage acknowledged by all the great names of the Labour movement, including Aneurin Bevan, Laski, Crosland, and Herbert Morrison. "Non-Marxists who, like myself, are not part of that tradition, firmly believe that we must preserve within our movement a place for those who are ..." And later: "I therefore hope ... the National Executive will not allow the fact that Andy Bevan declares himself to be a Marxist, to provide grounds for declaring him to be unsuitable to exercise his functions as a servant of the executive." In December 1976 Bevan was appointed the Labour Party's National Youth Officer.

Benn, a declared non-Marxist, lent his weight to Bevan in the full knowledge that Bevan was committed to an undemocratic form of socialism. So too did the NEC in the end. Entryism was being underwritten by the Left-dominated hierarchy of the Labour Party. Quite a different view of the threat was expressed not only by Shirley Williams but by Denis Healey, Roy Hattersley and virtually all the leading right-wing politicians within Labour.

The Bevan episode was all the more controversial following as it did the Underhill Report. This had been written a year previously in November 1975, but not made public. Reg Underhill, then national agent of the Labour Party, produced a report which for the first time investigated the phenomenon of entryism and the Militant Tendency. It was based on a forty-five page document produced by the Tendency and called 'British Perspectives and Tasks 1974'. It gave considerable cause for concern, but whilst the Right wished to publish and give the document wide circulation, the NEC refused to do so. It was not till 1980 that the NEC authorised publication. Though it was clear from the text that the Tendency was small, it was organised on a national basis, with central headquarters, full-time organisers and a national membership. In 1980 it was reported to have sixty-three full-time workers. Its propaganda was and is disseminated through its newspaper, *The Militant*.

The Tendency's aim was to infiltrate the party at all levels; the Young Socialists were to be the advance guard, the "spearhead in the trade unions and Labour Party wards and constituencies carrying the ideas of Marxism into the wards and constituencies, trade union branches, and shop steward committees."

In 1980, at the time when Labour finally agreed to publication, *The Times* wrote a leader under the heading 'The evidence they chose to ignore', asserting that there could be no justification for such secrecy and going on to suggest that the Militant Tendency offended the Party's Constitution which stipulates that people are not eligible for membership of the Labour Party if they also belong to political organisations "having their own programme, principles and policy for distinctive and separate propaganda, or possessing branches in the constituencies ...".

Since the legitimate Left, the Tribune Group, lacked a grassroots organisation, the Militants were successful in representing the Left in the constituency parties.

Though Communist Party members, unlike the Militants, cannot openly operate within the Labour Party, they have the right to be active within the trade union movement. The Communist Party, which has been in continuous decline in Britain since the war, has made great strides within the trade unions.

Stephen Milligan, journalist on the *Economist*, in his book about the unions, *The New Barons*, published in 1976, states: "The Communist Party is the only effective organisation within the trade union movement that tries to control the outcome of elections, and its success over the years has been remarkable, thanks to the wide-spread apathy among trade union members towards elections."

Milligan is also able to give more specific evidence of that success: at the time of the miners' dispute which brought down the Heath government in 1974, a quarter of the NUM's executive were communists, six out of twenty-four, and "there is a Communist Party member on nearly every union executive in Britain."

Although the presence of Communists in high places within the trade union movement has become an accepted feature of British society, it is an extraordinary concept. Quite openly, with the consent of the society involved, Communists are able to use their influence not only to improve the lot of trade unionists but to bring about an undemocratic, totalitarian society.

Trade unions have 90% of the votes at Conference. They have the majority voice in determining who is elected to the National Executive Committee. They sponsor 120 or so individual MPs. They have 40% of the votes in the election of Labour Party leaders and deputy leaders. The trade unions thus have the greatest influence on Labour policy and in deciding who gets the jobs of Leader and MP. Within the trade unions, therefore, the Communists have an influence disproportionate to their numbers.

So the leftward pressures within the Labour movement came from many quarters: from the Communists and the Trotskyites; from many legitimate, democratic sources within the Party, idealists of the old school like Fenner Brockway and Michael Foot, newer voices like those of Eric Heffer and Neil Kinnock preaching a democratic socialism, youthful idealists, as well as from many uncompromising socialists for whom, according to Shirley Williams, consent is a sort of optional extra.

The Labour Right, finding themselves swimming against the tide, either got out of the water, or made the motions of swimming while drifting with the current. It was an unhappy time. The atmosphere in the party was bad. The forces of democratic and undemocratic Left, though often competing with one another, combined to exert a continuous pressure on the social democratic and working class labourist elements in the Party.

As a small unit, the CLP could be infiltrated, and the Party's declining membership had resulted in many CLPs becoming smaller. The fifty or so remaining activists in many CLPs were often predominantly of the Left. In 1981, 85% of the CLPs voted for Tony Benn for the deputy leadership, reflecting accurately the tendency in the grassroots.

The CLPs' composition had changed. Where in the two decades after the war the people attending meetings had represented a cross-section of the locality, later they came from a much narrower stratum of society. The 1950s mix of postmen, factory workers, teachers, trade unionists, civil servants, bus drivers had changed. By the 1970s administrative, teaching, social and public sector staff predominated, while most of the manual or unskilled workers had disappeared. The bus drivers, the factory workers and the postmen dropped by the wayside. They did not share the vision of the new middle-class and uncompromising left-wingers. Hostility and dogma had soured the club atmosphere for them.

The party of tolerance became a place where moderates were shouted down, booed and hissed. Even the Left agrees that it was not the moderates who behaved in this way. According to one right-wing trade unionist: "If I was hissed I knew I must be talking sense." The uncommitted public, too, had the opportunity to hear the Labour Party 'debating' when television brought the Party and TUC conferences into their living rooms. The hissing and barracking of comrades within the movement seemed the manifestation of deeper ills beneath the surface.

Around this time, in the mid-seventies, the social democrats within Labour were at their lowest point. It would have been almost impossible to forecast that within only five or six years they would emerge as a fighting unit, declaring their independence, to carry on the social democratic struggle as a separate party. In the mid-seventies, the social democrats were on the run, disorientated, lacking the will and the power to fight back in a concerted way. They looked unlikely to become a major political force again, as they continued to compromise, and blend with the dominant Left.

The fact that they did take up the fight was as much due to others as to themselves. For the Left's campaign to introduce their form of party democracy was intended to give the Left permanent control of the Party. It was to be the decisive campaign where the winner was to take all. With their backs forced against the ropes, the social democrats finally had the resolve to fight back, though even at that late stage only a minority did so and then in fits and starts, with less than total conviction, as will be seen. It was not till the final months before the Limehouse Declaration that David Owen fought for the social democratic cause with the conviction previously lacking in the Labour Right's internal performance.

It should be mentioned that a number of Right campaigns were waged at this time, but each in its different way was less than convincing. Each responded to leftist pressures. Each aimed to promote popular progressive policies and broader party democracy based on members rather than activists only. There were three main campaigns.

The Manifesto Group had a membership of about ninety parliamentarians and was intended as a counterbalance to the Tribune Group of MPs, numbering a little under eighty. Its moderate MP members ran a worthy campaign, but effectiveness was strictly limited. In the words of one critical sympathiser, Manifesto was a typical 'wet' initiative.

More interesting was the sister grouping which campaigned through its members in the constituencies: the Campaign for Labour Victory. This was modelled on the earlier, successful Campaign for Democratic Socialism, also a grassroots organisation. But where the CDS had had a relatively easy assignment in steering a predominantly right-wing Labour Party back on course, the 1977 CLV had quite another problem: to swing back to the right a Labour Party which by now was further Left than ever before. Shirley Williams, Bill Rodgers, Ian Wrigglesworth and John Cartwright were amongst the MPs who backed the campaign.

Although CLV could not achieve its aim, it did form a kind of prototype for the Social Democratic Party and led naturally into it. Many of its members became founder members of the new party when it was formed in 1981. Its secretary, Alec McGivan became the first Secretary of the SDP. However, half CLV's membership was to soldier on inside the Labour Party.

The third right-wing campaign of this period was run by the Social Democratic Alliance. Founded in June 1975, two years before the Campaign for Labour Victory was launched, the SDA was the most uncompromising in its hostility to extremist trends inside the Party. Curiously, it established a somewhat extremist image itself, for to many sympathisers inside the party it often seemed too outspoken or even too right-wing. Yet its predominantly Labour members saw themselves as continuing the old Labour tradition. Though membership grew, it never achieved the influence it wished. Finally, when in 1980 the SDA decided to prepare lists of its supporters to contest parliamentary and council seats against extreme Left Labour candidates, it was proscribed.

It was thus the first group officially outlawed since the Labour Party ended proscription in 1973. Though the SDA had clearly transgressed the Party rules in its intention to compete with it, it was symptomatic of the trend of the previous decade that the first proscription should be of a right-wing group. Soon after the formation of the Social Democratic Party, the SDA chairman, Dr Stephen Haseler joined the new party's policy committee.

Many eminent people parted company with the Labour Party during the leftward years of the seventies. Among the more notable were politicians George Brown, Reg Prentice, Richard Marsh, Christopher Mayhew, Dick Taverne and Brian Walden, as well as former editor of the *New Statesman*, Paul Johnson. And Roy Jenkins and David Marquand resigned their seats and left for the international politics of Brussels and the European Commission.

Of the top echelon, only the moderates were leaving. Though these people were very different from one another, they had one thing in common: they had all had enough. There seemed no future for social democrats in the modern Labour Party.

Later, in 1980, George Brown was to become President of the SDA. In 1981 he became a member of the new party though not one of the leaders. It was not to be the Gang of Five. In July 1981 George Brown was canvassing for Jenkins at the Warrington by-election.

Dick Taverne dropped out of politics after his marginal defeat in the second of the two 1974 General Elections. He had had enough. In 1981, though he was keeping a low profile, he was back in politics on SDP platforms addressing large audiences. Those around him in the SDP assumed that he would emerge as one of the important figures in the Social Democratic Party.

Christopher Mayhew, ex-Navy minister and Labour MP more or less continuously since 1945, left the Party to join the Liberals in July 1974. He referred to a Labour Party "too vulnerable to the extreme Left and too dependent on the unions. I particularly support their the Liberals' campaign for a political re-alignment. We need a revolt of the centre against extremes. We must break away from the old Tory-Labour confrontation which sets one half of the country against the other." While the Prime Minister, Harold Wilson had joked in the House at the expense of the Liberals, referring to "the major and minor Tories", *The Times* leader, reporting the affair, put the Mayhew episode into another perspective: "Mr Mayhew has given Labour not a body blow but a warning." That warning was not to be taken. Mayhew was to lose his seat in the Commons. In due course, seven years later he was, as a Liberal, a founder member of the Alliance.

One man who left the Labour Party amidst considerable controversy and who was not eventually to make his way into either SDP or the Alliance was Reg Prentice. A former cabinet minister, he had had a running battle with his constituency over many years and a growing struggle with Wilson, who was careful not to back him. Many would say Wilson was proved right when Prentice did the unspeakable - crossed the floor of the House, soon to become a Conservative Cabinet Minister in Mrs Thatcher's government. The former Labour Minister for Education and Science became a Conservative Minister of Social Security with responsibility for the disabled.

Prentice's desertion to the enemy camp stemmed from his analysis of the political trend: "There has been growing emphasis on class war and Marxist dogma ... There are only two real options - a Labour Government much more extreme than ever before, or a Conservative Government under Margaret Thatcher."

The dispute in Prentice's constituency, Newham North East, had been a running sore in the Labour movement. Prentice had made himself a target for left-wing activists through the public utterances in which he deplored trade unions setting themselves up against the law, even when that law stemmed from the Heath government. Neither did he endear himself by criticising the unions for their behaviour under the Social Contract with the Labour government: they should not "welsh" on their promises, he said.

By 1975, the Newham North East Labour Party dismissed Prentice as their future candidate. The affair rumbled on with a vigorous fight back by Prentice and his supporters until 1977. Prentice later wrote in his essay 'Right Turn' that "the Left had been reinforced, particularly by several Trotskyists of the so-called Militant Tendency, some of whom moved into Newham to secure my overthrow. The really disturbing aspect of Trotskyist infiltration into the Labour Party is that they are so readily accepted by other left-wingers, whose outlook is not very different ... they the Trotskyists provide a cutting edge for a much wider group of the Left, who follow their lead." *

---

* In the collection of essays of the same name, edited by Patrick Cormack, published by Leo Cooper, 1978

Prentice's move to the Tories made his active supporters bitter. John Cartwright, founder member of the SDP, vice-chairman at that time of the Manifesto Group said: "I cannot understand for the life of me, however disenchanted he was with the Labour Party, that he should cross the floor of the House." For the Left, and indeed, for many Labour people, Prentice was simply a traitor to the cause.

The significance of the Newham North East affair was the spotlight it had directed on the continuing and hardening influence of the Left. By 1977 the Marxist influence alongside that of the democratic Left could no longer be ignored. The background to the dispute was Labour's Programme 1976 and its underlying dogma which was steering the Party forward, a programme somewhat to the left, not only of Gaitskellite policies of old, but even of the Italian Communist Party's programme.

The Newham affair also gave fuel to the Left's insistence on new party procedures for the re-selection of MPs, and thus to the whole debate about party democracy, the Left's chosen instrument for gaining control of the Party. Party democracy was to be the caesarian operation which ensured that Social Democracy took up its own independent existence. Prentice and Newham North East had an inadvertent influence in bringing about an earlier, though scarcely premature birth.

PART IV

COUNT-DOWN
TO LABOUR PARTY SPLIT

Chapter Fifteen

THE MAKE-OR-BREAK ISSUE: PARTY DEMOCRACY

The popular satirical television programme *Not the Nine O'Clock News* once made its own comment on the idiosyncracies of democracy: five trade unionists holding a meeting decide to take a break. The first four put their hands up for tea, the fifth for coffee. Result: they all drink coffee, for the last man represents five million members, enough to settle the matter democratically!

The problem about democracy is that there are many ways of defining it. One man's democracy is another man's victimisation. The trade union block vote is one of the more controversial aspects, and the broader issue of party democracy no less so.

Accountability to the majority is what the Labour Party dispute was about. But which majority? Accountability to Party activists only? Accountability to all registered members of the Labour Party? Or accountability to the electorate? To take a parallel: does a school which sets out to be 'democratic' look to its teachers (activists) for support, or additionally to its pupils (all members), or parents and broader community (voters) as well? The final definition of democracy determines the nature of the Labour Party and effectively who runs it, hence the intensity of the debate.

The Left had three main planks in its campaign for party democracy. First, that MPs should be more accountable to their constituency Labour parties. Second, that the Party, through Conference and the NEC, should be the final arbiter of policy, and third, that the leader and deputy leader should be elected by the Party as a whole. These objectives had one common aim: to make Labour MPs and ministers accountable to the national Party. At the root of the Left's initiative lay a breakdown of trust in its representatives.

It is true that Labour MPs were more right-wing than the movement as a whole and, to that extent, not wholly representative. Though it needs to be said that the composition of Labour in the House had also been moving leftward. In 1976, when Harold Wilson resigned, left-winger Michael Foot won a sizeable percentage of MPs' votes in the election for Prime Minister. He won the largest number of votes on the first ballot and was within eight votes of Callaghan on the second. Indeed, in 1980 he was to become Leader in the last such election, with only Labour MPs voting.

War having been declared on the issue of Party democracy, the Right had to respond. Twelve right-wing Labour MPs, 'The Dirty Dozen', of whom half were to become first-wave Social Democrat MPs, wrote in *The Times*: "Rather than cling desperately to the sinking life raft of the *status quo*, we should now be saying with all our heart: 'Yes, we do need to change, to get up-to-date, to bring some real democracy and vitality back to our proceedings'." The Right sought to widen the concept of democracy - first, because this was more democratic, and second, because it furthered its own interests. For the Right's support lay not amongst the narrow band of activists, but among the broad membership and the electorate. Over the years, opinion polls had consistently indicated that voters and the broader Labour membership identified with the Labour Right's moderate policies although there were, of course, exceptions. For example, more often than not, the electorate preferred the Left's anti-Common Market stance. But overall the Right's vision was the more acceptable. Hence the Left's unwillingness to broaden its campaign for democracy. Hence the fundamental flaw in democracy on its terms. If the Left had considered that the broader democracy would win votes, it would have sought it.

The flaw in the Right's campaign was a different one. Why had it been content to accept the imperfections of the existing system and only fight for change when challenged by the Left's campaign? The answer was simply that the old system had worked. Whatever its inadequacies, as long as the PLP and trade unions had agreed on policies broadly reflecting the electorate's mood, all went well. Problems only arose after the Left altered the balance of the Labour movement.

A number of overlapping campaigns have been waged by the Left with great vigour and considerable success since the Campaign for Labour Party Democracy was formed in 1973 during the years of opposition. In 1978 the influential Labour Co-ordinating Committee, under the chairmanship of Tony Benn's right-hand man, the minister Michael Meacher, got under way. Just before the special conference of May 1980 at Wembley, nine left-wing pressure groups came together to form the Rank and File Mobilising Committee: these included both the groups just mentioned (CLPD and LCC), the Socialist Campaign for Labour Victory, Institute for Workers' Control, Independent Labour Publications, National Organisation of Labour Students and Clause 4, and later also the Labour Party Young Socialists and the Militant Tendency.

The Left's first success was on mandatory re-selection of MPs. Henceforth, whether CLPs were happy with their MPs' representation or not, MPs would have to be re-selected willy-nilly in mid-term between general elections. In spite of the Right's fierce campaign that this should be in the hands of all members of the constituency parties, on a one-member-one-vote basis, the Left won. Re-selection would be the responsibility of activists only, or as Ian Mikardo said: "It is the democracy of the committed, of the ones that really do the work." This was a major victory on two counts: an MP could be dropped or he could be 'persuaded' to toe the CLP line to ensure he stayed. In 1981, surprisingly, almost all MPs were re-selected under the new procedure. However, when it came to voting in the deputy leadership elections, many were leaned upon by their local party: the CLP's displeasure had become a potent weapon.

The Right's only, and many thought temporary, victory was in staving off Party control of the manifesto. Clause 5 of the Labour Party's constitution would continue to apply. Party and Cabinet (or Shadow Cabinet) would agree jointly on priority for policies, with the Cabinet taking final responsibility. Benn challenged this in November 1981. In a speech in the House, he deviated from Shadow Cabinet policy, harking back to an earlier Conference vote, and found himself in trouble with the Leader Michael Foot and most of his parliamentary colleagues on Left and Right.

The Left, however, emerged triumphant on the third plank of its policy for party reform. Election of the leader was to be the responsibility not of the PLP as previously, but of an electoral college representing the Labour movement as a whole. Although the PLP and the right wing would have preferred 'no change', they campaigned hard on the one-member-one-vote electoral college. David Owen in particular had decided that this was to be the final issue on which appeasement had to stop. The composition of the college was not finally resolved till the special conference on 24 January 1981. The outcome was a humiliation for the PLP whose share

119

of the votes was to be 30%, the CLPs' another 30%, with the largest share of 40% going to the trade unions.

That was the signal for the first break. The next day, the Gang of Four released their Limehouse Declaration, protesting at the move away from parliamentary control. The Council for Social Democracy had been born.

It must be said that the unions' 40% share had been arrived at as a compromise solution. Neither the Left nor the Right had really intended the unions to have the lion's share. Nor was it a good advertisement for democracy, since the trade union block vote was suspect as a democratic mechanism. Fistly, not all trade unionists were Labour Party members or even sympathisers. Many were Communists, many Conservatives, others Liberals, Nationalists or from other parties. Thus, a substantial non-Labour Party union membership would be influencing the Labour leadership. Secondly, the block vote was subject to manipulation and 'fixing in smoke-filled rooms', as the horror stories go, or as the Limehouse Declaration expressed it: "A handful of trade union leaders can now dictate the choice of a future Prime Minister."

The argument was to go on raging. Long term, the Left wanted changes such as accountability of local councillors to the CLP apparatus, the abolition of the House of Lords, and the election of cabinet ministers rather than appointment by the Prime Minister. Benn argued that "any patronage system is inherently corrupting to donor and donee alike".

The Right wanted a restructured NEC to include MPs and local councillors in their own right, with CLPs sending separately grassroots representatives; it wanted the local party membership to have greater influence in the CLPs.

The Tribune Group had started the ball rolling in 1972 with its pamphlet 'Labour - Party or Puppet?'. Many of its aims had been achieved. Now it was the turn of Members of Parliament to ask: 'Labour - MPs or puppets?'. For with mandatory re-selection had come a fundamental change in the relation between MPs and their party. The oldest principle of parliamentary democracy was involved: whether an MP was to use his judgement to represent all his constituents, or be mandated by his party to do as it instructed.

The party supremacy which was being imposed had three drawbacks. First, whatever the terminology, party democracy was the opposite of democratic. It was a step on the road to party control East European style, with the party hierarchy as the new elite. Second, party supremacy on the terms of the Left ensured policies and a style unacceptable to the majority of the electorate: the electorate had consistently indicated that it rejected narrow dogma. And third, the Left's unrelenting drive for and successful attainment of party democracy itself forced those who were loth to leave the party to do so. Thus the Left's success created the Social Democratic Party.

The Labour Left had won a pyrrhic victory. Its heritage was a weakened Party which was leaking MPs and members at an alarming rate. Even more important, its electoral support was being eroded: Warrington, Croydon, Crosby and a host of council by-elections were to prove that. Gerald Kaufman's observation rings true: you can fix a general management committeee, you can fix a constituency party, you can even fix a conference - but the one thing you cannot fix is the electorate.

In another context, Bertolt Brecht wrote: "Would it then not really be simpler if the Government dissolved the people and elected another?" *

---

* Brecht poem, written 1953, published posthumously

Chapter Sixteen

1979-81: STEEP ROAD TO LIMEHOUSE

When, in May 1979, the Labour Party lost the General Election, there was a major post-mortem. The Party at large, which by 1979 was mainly composed of a left-wing membership, was convinced that once again the Parliamentary Labour Party was to blame.

Here was a Labour movement which consistently voted for radical measures at annual conferences, and there the PLP which opted for a watered-down version. Why, for example, was the decision, overwhelmingly carried, that the House of Lords should be abolished, not included in the election manifesto? Red-blooded left wingers were scarcely going to be satisfied with the 1979 manifesto or agree with its title, 'The Labour Way is the better way', if all it said on this was: "We propose ... to abolish the delaying power and legislative veto of the House of Lords."

Later Tony Benn was to make a dramatic appeal to Conference (Blackpool 1980) by suggesting that within three weeks of Labour next taking office, 1,000 peers would be created to vote the establishment out of existence. The suggestion was greeted with both enthusiasm and derision: Harold Wilson and Shirley Williams could not help but wonder why it would take Tony so long, when it had taken God only six days to create the world.

The difficulty about party manifestos is that, for the activist, they should incorporate Labour policy, based on Conference decisions. At the same time they have to be acceptable to the PLP, whose members have to promote and defend them before the electorate. Often the difference is one of emphasis. Not so, however, in 1979. The argument about this manifesto was to flare up again two years after Labour's defeat.

Tony Benn had himself been a member of the Labour Cabinet for eleven years and during that time, as has been pointed out by his opponents on both the Right and Left, he never chose to resign. After 1979 he consistently attacked the record of the late Labour Government. He also claimed that agreed policy had been omitted deliberately from the Party manifesto. This led to a unique exchange with the Chief Whip, Michael Cocks: "This is the first time that I have ever spoken about my work in public because the tradition has been for the Chief Whip to maintain a low profile." However, he became so incensed by Benn's allegations that he not only spoke out against them but made a tape-recording, comparing Benn's allegations with the actual text of the 1979 manifesto. The tape was for distribution to all constituency parties. Though it was an amateur effort, put together with the help of Cocks' friend, Councillor Len Smith, and his daughter, the discrepancy between Benn's allegations and the manifesto text was quite clear. Wealth tax, increase in public expenditure, cuts in arms spending - none had been omitted. Cocks' efforts did not, however, kill the arguments.

Above all, the extra-parliamentary Party blamed the Labour Government directly for the loss of the election. Labour activists saw the 1974-79 Labour Government as conservative and pusillanimous - in the tradition of the earlier model of 1964-70. A decade earlier, back-bencher Michael Foot, during his unsuccessful fight for the deputy leadership of the party against Roy Jenkins, after electoral defeat in mid-1970, wrote: "What is needed is a strong shift leftwards. The Party in Parliament ought to start that process and, if it won't, the Party conference will have to do it for them." A major shift to the left occurred in 1979 as it did then.

The NEC had been moving leftwards over the last fifteen years. While in 1964 it comprised twenty right-wingers and only eight from the Left, by the time of the 1979 election, the balance was reversed: eighteen from the Left and eleven from the Right.

Now the new refrain was accountability. The PLP must become accountable to the movement. So must the leader. The Cabinet must be accountable. Likewise local councillors. Never again must the PLP and those elected become so independent of the Party outside that its policies become watered down to a pale shadow of Conference decisions.

The Callaghan/Healey axis in particular was under attack. Callaghan, who had previously prided himself on his ability to understand the unions and get on with them, found himself increasingly on the defensive. In particular, his final decision to postpone the election from the autumn of 1978 to

May 1979 was seen as disastrous.

The winter of discontent which followed has become hallowed as a phrase. It was a season of unions in revolt against the Government's incomes policy. The 5% increase put forward as the wage settlement norm proved unacceptable. The union leaders had warned that the membership would not agree and were proved right. Strikes rather than 5% become the norm.

While the Labour Right blamed the unions, the Left blamed Callaghan and Healey for stepping out of line, for arrogance and independence, for not following Labour guidelines, and finally for being just plain wrong. Although *Tribune* wrote the following at a later date, it would have rung equally true at the time: "... there is no truth in the rumour that Denis Healey has been admitted to hospital while doctors carry out tests to see if they can find any trace of Labour Party policy."

For the same reason the *New Statesman* opposed the idea that Healey should become leader of the Party one day. The depth of hostility to centre-right Labour government, and to Healey personally, can be judged from the paper's editorial: "If there is one thing more likely to wreck the Labour Party than two decades of Wilson/Callaghan, it is three decades of Wilson/Callaghan/Healey rule."

Yet, as Labour back-bencher, Frank Hooley has pointed out, during the only session in the 1974 to 1979 Government when Labour had a majority over all other parties, Labour put on the statute book no less than eighty-three Acts implementing a wide range of manifesto promises, including employment protection, child benefits, education reforms, three housing acts, the creation of the National Enterprise Board, three acts covering industrial injuries, others dealing with oil taxation, pensions, prices, sex discrimination, five social security acts, several consumer protection acts and the creation of the Scottish and Welsh Development Agencies.

Nevertheless, in the words of one SDP MP: "The Party at large wanted to repudiate all the Government's work. They want to re-write history." So the Left saw defeat and policies not carried out, while others in the Party saw the implementation of progressive legislation. But it was the Left which was making the running. The Right was left to draw its own conclusions - either to move a step further left in the Labour spectrum or to take the fight back into the Left's camp.

There was another alternative: to leave politics altogether. Many Labour supporters were by this time very disillusioned. They thought that Labour had been unlikely to win the 1979 election, and were not surprised when it lost. A former parliamentary candidate and chairman of a constituency Labour party for many years explained how he felt then: "I was deeply depressed. I was ashamed. I was having to defend the unions. Unofficial strikes were being made official by a weak leadership, leading from behind. At least Scanlon and Jack Jones had been men with backbone, but the new leaders were so transparently not in control. Ambulance drivers jeopardising lives, grave-diggers striking. My gut feeling told me the unions had too much influence. It was at this time that I seriously considered leaving politics."

As well as this unease about the unions, there was also a feeling that the Party had run out of ideas. So thought former Labour Minister, John Horam, one of the first MPs to cross over to the Social Democrats. So did others. Left activists thought the Government had not been radical enough. Right-wingers like Horam agreed, but for rather different reasons: "Speaking as an economist, what bothered me was that we were not going anywhere. Our analysis was shaky and you do need an analysis. Labour was merely keeping disaster at bay under IMF pressure, while being squeezed between old ideas like nationalisation and the dead weight of the trade unions. The sheer conservatism of the party made it tough to make headway. We were not making use of a whole range of economic weapons, devising new concepts to make the economy grow. Keynes was right when he said 'Ideas are central to politics'. Life for us Social Democrats locked into the party had become an intellectual ghetto."

Although, as Horam says, even before the rash of trade union strikes in the winter of 1978/9 Labour could no longer give the country a strong lead, he still needed some months to draw the appropriate conclusion. In his early political career, Horam had contributed critical articles to the left-wing *Tribune* magazine and had voted against entry into Europe. He was now searching for radical solutions on the right of the party spectrum.

For Dick Taverne, Labour's defeat in May 1979 was the moment of a new opportunity. The picture originally painted by him depicted Labour losing in the first 1974 election. The flag which he had been holding aloft alone in Lincoln, would then be taken up by others, the Party would have split and the two pieces gone their separate ways. In the event, Labour won and Taverne's scenario evaporated.

To Taverne, the breakdown of the Social Contract was another signal which might have led to a split in the Party. With wage claims up to 80% per year, and settlements coming through at 38%, inflation had risen to an all-time monthly high of betweeen 30% and 40%. Jack Jones' belated influence on an incomes policy saved the day. Callaghan had then taken over as Prime Minister and "made politics more honest again".

The May 1979 election could resurrect Taverne's original scenario. By the autumn, for a growing number of Labour moderates, the split began to look more likely.

The 1979 conference came as something of a shock to those in the party who always assumed that "all will come right in the end". For here they were attending a fraternal gathering where clearly the divisions had widened, resulting in considerable hostility. Here in Brighton, against a backcloth of so much architectural beauty, a drama was enacted which, to many participants, was ugly.

Michael Foot's promise following the 1970 election defeat was coming true: Conference was indeed helping the Party in Parliament to embark on a strong leftward tilt. To many participants, the spirit in which this was enacted was as depressing as the shift itself.

MPs were in the firing line. In attendance only as ex-officio members, they came under continuous attack. The Party had lost the election and the Members of Parliament were to blame. One of the participants there recalls: "I have never seen MPs savaged in this way. MPs were being attacked even by the platform, by Ron Hayward and others."

"It was," said another "reminiscent of the Cultural Revolution. They were trying to wipe the slate clean. If they had gone along with the idea that, broadly, the Labour Government had been doing or trying to do the right things, but it was just the opposite. A total repudiation. My party of decency was transformed into a mob of snarling Red Guards shouting class motivated comments."

No allowances were made for the constraints under which the government had operated, that it had no majority in the House from November 1976 onwards, that for eighteen months, between February 1977 and the autumn of 1978, it had had to work within the confines of a Lib-Lab pact and that surviving itself was an achievement.

One fundamental issue affecting Members of

Parliament, which had repeatedly been put before Conference, was now decided. The principle of compulsory re-selection of MPs was carried two to one, though this new procedure was again to come before Conference the following year. The main victory for making parliamentarians accountable had been won.

As a result of this vote, Members of Parliament would be very much more closely tied to the local party apparatus, i.e. the party activists. This was in direct opposition to the recommendation of the Right, such as the parliamentary Manifesto group and the broader-based Campaign for Labour Victory who wanted the constituency membership at large to have more control, instead of restricting accountability to a handful of hard-core ideologues. It was now to be mandatory for an MP to come up for re-selection within three years of a general election, and no MP would henceforth be able to assume re-selection as of right: in safe seats in the Labour heartlands, an MP could no longer settle down to a career for life without repeated self-justification.

It was the first success of the Left for tighter party control. It culminated with the January 1981 special Wembley conference, convened to determine the composition of the electoral college (for electing Labour leaders).

The autumn conference, fifteen months before the Limehouse Declaration and nearly eighteen months before the new party came into existence, was the signal for new social democratic initiatives.

John Horam invited William Rodgers to lunch. Horam had been number two to the latter when Rodgers held the Transport portfolio in the Labour Government up to six months previously. Now Horam simply suggested it was time for the party to split. For Rodgers, according to Horam's understanding, this was a turning point. Certainly Rodgers made an important speech shortly afterwards, a milestone on the road to Social Democracy.

According to Taverne, some of the best-known people in the Labour ranks now felt that a split was not only likely but desirable. Some of these subsequently crossed to the Social Democrats. Others remain well-known names in the Labour Party.

Within a week of the conference ending, Clive Lindley, who in 1981 became a member of the Social Democratic steering committee, also decided it was time for action. He made contact with the Liberals. He sought out Roger

127

Pincham, whom he had fought as Labour candidate in the rural constituency of Leominster. In February 1974, Pincham had come within 579 votes of winning the seat for the Liberals.

Pincham, national chairman of the Liberal Party, and Lindley found that they had a lot in common. Lindley now says: "I implied I came as a representative of a large block of social democrats within the Labour Party and that I was some sort of an emissary of Roy Jenkins, neither of which was strictly true. I had come, I said, for the social democrats, to find some sort of accommodation with the Liberals, not to join them. I also suggested that our support in Leominster could be decisive and help Pincham win the seat, which by now he had contested four times." This discussion went well and led to a series of meetings of Liberals and social democrats. Lindley also promoted the social democratic cause through the Campaign for Labour Victory.

CLV, one of those groupings within Labour which exists from time to time to promote a specific political cause, had been in existence since 1977 and now, after the May 1979 defeat, it became more active with 4,000 or so people up and down the country promoting moderate Labour views. Unlike the Manifesto Group which comprised only MPs, CLV had a mainly grassroots membership of moderate activists, councillors and trade union members, with a sprinkling of MPs.

On 13 November 1979, the CLV steering committee wrote confidential letters to Bill Rodgers, Roy Hattersley and Roy Mason. They attached a document appraising the social democratic situation within the Party. And a very unhappy document it was. It stressed the lack of leadership from heavyweights in the Party, and appealed not only to these three but also to David Owen and Shirley Williams. "Committed social democrats feel completely leaderless ... occasional speeches are no longer enough"; a contrast was made with the Left's leadership where Tony Benn was "a major asset".

Ideologically, the CLV saw itself adrift, for lack of leadership. There was a total absence of "some coherent ideological structure". The result of this vacuum was a crumbling of the grassroots of the party. "Many of our people are now, for the first time in their lives, talking of the break-up of the Party. Frankly it is not just that they think it may happen - they actually believe it ought to happen... When one looks at the records of Party commitment of some of those who hold such views, it is clear what a deeply profound decision they have been forced to make."

Three of the four signatories of the CLV letter became founder members of the Social Democrats. Alec McGivan, the organising secretary of the CLV took on the same job for the new party, acting as agent for Roy Jenkins at the Warrington by-election in July 1981. Jim Daly became a member of the SDP's first steering committee. It is equally interesting to note that of the three recipients of the CLV letter, Rodgers was the only one to become a leader of the Social Democrats, while Hattersley and Mason stayed where they were.

Rodgers' reaction to the CLV document was mixed, though on the whole favourable. On 15 November, he wrote a carefully considered three-page letter, the gist of which was that the CLV should not expect too much. He compared it with the Campaign for Democratic Socialism of twenty years before, when "we took the lead ourselves without excessive reference to others."

On the lack of a specific ideology, Rodgers replied: "You simply expect too much. Social democrats should be wary of instant formulae", and suggested that the CLV talent could have a go themselves: "What prevents a new generation writing pamphlets and books? Crosland wrote the *Future of Socialism* in his thirties and when he was out of Parliament. Don't expect too much from the ageing warhorses of politics." On CLV's main point of leadership Rodgers wrote "... I can only speak for myself in saying that I am very happy to lead if you want!"

Rodgers was to give a lead later that month. On 30 November 1979 he made a speech to the Abertillery Constituency Labour Party as guest at their annual dinner. In it he gave the Party a year to put its house in order, making a call to arms that moderates could heed. In the event, he was only about two months out in his forecast, for within fourteen months he had signed the Limehouse Declaration, thereby bringing the Council for Social Democracy into existence.

The Abertillery speech was an important step toward Limehouse. Rodgers made his own position clear and provided a time-scale within which to work, a perspective on which to focus. It also represented the kind of leadership the CLV had been asking for - tough, eloquent, unambiguous.

"Our Party has a year - not much longer - in which to save itself. A year in which to start repairing its ramshackle organisation and to get some money in the till. A year to start

winning friends amongst the men and women - almost thirty
million of them - who did not vote Labour last time. A year in
which to start proving that it is a credible alternative to the
harsh and divisive government of Mrs Thatcher."

Rodgers went on: "But the omens are not good",
referring to the single view promoted by the NEC. "Its
exponents" he says, "want to clip the wings of Members of
Parliament. They want to choose a leader who will do their
bidding and conform to their requirements. They want to
dominate the manifesto-making process at election time ..."

A party of the far left - in which Tribune members would
be the moderates - would have little appeal to the millions of
voters who reject doctrinaire and extreme solutions ..."

"I do not believe that many of us would want to be a
passenger on such a gravy train to disaster.

"... If the hard-line leaders of the Left want a fight to the
finish, they can have it. But if as a result they should split the
Party, they should not suppose that the inheritance will be
theirs.

"... If our Party should abandon these principles, it
would be a tragedy. But they would not die. They would
survive because there would be men and women prepared to
carry on the fight.

"... It is for our Party itself to choose. I hope deeply that
it will stay true to its great tradition and continue to be the
best means of building the good society."

If Rodgers was a leader found by his followers, there was
another leader on the scene looking for followers. That same
month, Roy Jenkins, President of the Commission in Brussels,
former Deputy Leader of the Labour Party, was in London to
give the Dimbleby lecture. This lecture, given annually in
memory of the popular television broadcaster Richard
Dimbleby, provided Jenkins with the platform to sound out
public opinion in a country from which he had been absent for
four years. The response was immediate; he had clearly struck
a chord. Through many hundreds of letters, Jenkins learnt
that the troops were waiting to assemble. The Dimbleby
lecture was a key point on the road to Social Democracy.
Before and after 'Dimbleby' became the BC and AD of Social
Democracy.

Roy Jenkins argued for a "strengthening of the radical
centre" in British politics, believing that "such a development
could bring into political commitment the energies of many
people of talent and good will who, although perhaps active in

other voluntary ways, are alienated from the business of government, whether national or local, by the sterility and formalism of much of the political game."

In support of proportional representation, Jenkins maintained that the case for it was now overwhelming: "It is clearly a fairer system, accepted as such by the great majority of democratic countries." He was not afraid of coalitions, should it lead to that. It was the type of coalition which was decisive, not the principle. Incompatible coalitions were the ones to be avoided but "do we really believe that the last Labour Government was not a coalition, in fact if not in name, and a pretty incompatible one at that? I served in it for half its life and you could not convince me of anything else ..."

"I would much rather that it meant overt and compatible coalition than that it locked incompatible people, and still more important, incompatible philosophies, into a loveless, debilitating marriage, even if consecrated in a common tabernacle."

The main issue was to unfreeze the pattern of British politics. Jenkins affirmed his belief that "the electorate can tell 'a hawk from a handsaw' and that if it saw a new grouping with cohesion and relevant policies, it might be more attracted by this new reality than by old labels which had become increasingly irrelevant."

Faced with internecine warfare as the major purpose of a party's life, slogging through an unending war of attrition and defending as much of the old citadel as can be held is not the best response. Better to break out and mount a battle on new and higher ground.

Criticism of Jenkins' thesis was not slow in coming. In an assortment of reactions published in *The Listener*, for example, the attacks were fierce, many coming from eminent left-wingers.

Professor Bernard Crick expressed the view that "centrist moderation is not the key to economic recovery, it is part of the explanation for decline", believing it unlikely that "we will relapse to Mr Jenkins' favourite project of a dialectic marriage of Asquith and Attlee." As for Mr Jenkins' wish for "the innovating stimulus of the free market without unacceptable brutality", Crick draws his own conclusion: "and we need camels without smell and with feathers."

Neil Kinnock spoke disparagingly of "the gaggle of Labour Party 'exitists' now joined by Roy Jenkins. From the vantage-points of the House of Lords, assorted boardrooms, or the top of the butter mountain, they show us a new heaven and a new earth.''

Enoch Powell saw Jenkins' ideas for Britain's recovery as unrealistic political electro-convulsive therapy.

But a positive response was equally immediate. Jenkins had judged correctly. Councillors, trade unionists, Labour voters, Conservatives unhappy about the early days of the Thatcher administration, people who had a high regard for him personally, all contacted Roy Jenkins to offer their moral or active support. Precisely the sort of grassroots mix of activists and voters needed to breathe life into any future radical grouping of the centre.

One of those who picked up the telephone within days of the lecture was Jim Daly, Senior Lecturer in politics at North East London Polytechnic. Daly had been Chairman of GLC Transport while GLC Councillor from 1973 to 1977. He had stood as Labour candidate in the first European elections in June, and been defeated in the landslide of Tory victories, but not before being appalled by the ambiguous nature of central Labour Party support for him as an official Labour Europe candidate. So Daly, executive member of the London Labour Party, telephoned Brussels and to his surprise, in spite of all the stories of layers of bureaucracy there, was put straight through to Jenkins' office.

Daly's offer of help was particularly constructive. He proposed that Jenkins should be supplied with regular information about what was going on in the UK; Jenkins would be kept in touch with what was happening behind the scenes through considered commentaries and relevant press clippings.

To achieve this, Daly offered to run 'The Radical Centre for Democratic Studies in Industry and Society', whose sole function would in effect be to service one man - Roy Jenkins in Brussels. "We, at the Centre, will provide you with a political secretariat."

Daly, Clive Lindley and John Morgan, the television journalist, funded the Centre jointly, and Daly ran it meticulously from his Chiswick home. The Centre had no members and needed little money. What was needed was provided by Daly and Lindley personally. "I did not mind", says Daly, "turning over my lecture and consultancy fees, if the money was actually going to do something useful." Jenkins accepted the offer and was kept informed. In his turn, he kept in touch with Daly and his colleagues.

This devotion to the new party, even before it existed, was an accurate forerunner of the subsequent phenomenon of people of all ranks jostling for the opportunity to help the cause quite selflessly.

Jenkins also kept in touch with a whole network of like-minded people: David Steel; the Social Democratic Alliance; David Marquand, Professor of Contemporary History and Politics at Salford University, former Labour MP and biographer of Ramsay MacDonald, who had worked at the Commission and was particularly close to Jenkins; Lord Harris of Greenwich, and Dick Taverne. Others with whom he had contact were known in the interests of anonymity as 'the Group'. Its purpose was to prepare for the new party.

The first meeting of potential social democratic recruits took place soon after "Dimbleby" at the home of Colin Phipps who had been Labour MP for Dudley West. Those present included David Marquand, Dick Taverne and Michael Barnes - all, like the host, former Labour MPs. Also present were John Horam, then in the House working as Shadow Financial Spokesman under Healey, Tom Clitheroe, one of three councillors from the Midlands who had left the Labour Party, Clive Lindley and a number of others. For the sake of secrecy, no minutes were kept.

This group, although unified in its wish to create a new social democratic party, did not agree on its tactics and soon strong differences of opinion began to form. Two schools of thought emerged: the 'let's go now' approach and the 'slowly, slowly catchee monkey' approach.

The first faction, consisting of Phipps and Barnes and supported by the Social Democratic Alliance, thought that they should break out of the Labour Party now. An embryo organisation should be set up which could act as a magnet for Labour MPs, to make defection easier and more attractive for MPs and others; the way must be prepared for party refugees. Its creation should precede the autumn conference which would inevitably create new pressures on moderates from the Left.

A slow approach was favoured by Lord Harris, Clive Lindley and others, and by Jenkins himself, and this view prevailed. Quite simply, it was thought that Shirley Williams and Bill Rodgers were crucial to the success of the new party, and worth waiting for. Both were now seen as 'hawkish'.The Group could work towards this goal without impediment, whereas going public would mean that Williams and Rodgers would have to oppose them. By mid-1980 the Group had split.

Also in mid-year, another significant milestone was passed when the grassroots conference of the Campaign for Labour Victory was held in Birmingham on 10 and 11 May. About eighty people attended. The main speakers were Shirley Williams, Bill Rodgers and David Owen.

For the first time in a Labour Party forum, the alternative of a new social democratic party was discussed openly. During the week-end conference, it became clear what the breaking point for different individuals might be. Both Shirley Williams and Bill Rodgers gave considerable encouragement in their platform speeches. In this heady atmosphere the odd person out on the platform was David Owen. He clearly felt concerned at being caught up in this climate of rising mutiny to which, at that stage, he was prepared to lend neither his leadership nor even his participation. He expressed the view that such discussions would undermine the moderate wing's position within Labour and burden it with a lack of credibility in the fight within the Labour Party. He saw a fight to win over the Party to the moderate view taking a whole decade until 1990.

At present, Owen said, he was ready to attack those who considered there was an alternative in a centre party. Within a few months, Owen had swung round completely and had become the toughest of the dissident leaders.

However, David Owen did at this stage make it clear that he had a breaking point: an unacceptable Party manifesto would bring him to this. There was a danger that the manifesto would have many unacceptable aspects: anti-EEC, anti-NATO, pro-unilateral disarmament, anti-market forces, anti-private enterprise, anti-incomes policy, deeply centralist, anti-police, paying lip-service to Third World problems while adopting protectionist policies.

For the present, speaker after speaker expressed weariness at the thought of years of further infighting. As Jim Daly, the first that week-end to get up and say he was ready to leave the Party, now recalls: "Owen gave me a pretty cold shoulder that week-end. He thought I was a wild man, guilty of treasonable talk."

Daly referred to a Labour Party that goes on indulging in internal enmities, to the sheer unadulterated boredom of sitting through meetings dominated by discussions of an almost unbelievable inanity, to the impossibility of dealing with not only the dedicated Marxists and Trotskyists, but also the 'Trendy Radicals' and the 'Jill Tweedie Left', and he finally declared that if Roy Jenkins came back from Europe to set up a new party then that is where he, Jim Daly, would be going!

Trevor Lindley, Roy Mason's agent who became a member of the Social Democrats in June 1981, talked of the struggle in Scargill territory, in "the people's republic of South Yorkshire."

Similar voices represented half the conference. Others were for continuing the struggle inside Labour. All considered the moderates' position difficult and weak.

If for some Owen's words came as a cold shower, the positive approach of Williams and Rodgers was a real encouragement. Social Democrats inside the Labour Party remembered the Abertillery speech, and waited for confirmation that Rodgers was still on course. Rodgers now spoke openly about a fourth party.

"Unless we in CLV win a considerable victory and show that we have a momentum to bring the Party back, I believe that it will lead to a party in the centre of the political spectrum being formed." Much would depend on Roy Jenkins, whether he felt the Labour Party had gone beyond redemption and whether he raised "a banner outside the Party". As to the Party's future, there was little room for optimism.

Shirley Williams' view coincided with Rodgers', not with Owen's. She saw the outcome being decided within one to two years, not ten. Labour's draft manifesto had horrified her since it was totally unrealistic and would reduce the Party to the status of opposition party and no more. On the one hand the draft document "looks forward to the prosperity of the 1980s." On the other it demonstrates a Maginot line mentality based on state control and isolationism both economic and political, half committing the Party to pull out of NATO and the EEC.

If the Labour Party was impossibly unrealistic in its policies or behaving unacceptably, and as a result had no hope of winning elections without the help of the social democrats, then she didn't wish to be part of that scenario. She was quite prepared to accept that without the social democrats there would never be another Labour Government.

Within three weeks of the CLV meeting, on 1 June, a special Labour Party conference was held in Wembley. This was the first of three conferences to be held within the space of eight months, a frequency unmatched in Party history. These conferences were concerned with the formulation of policies, not to oppose the traditional enemy without - the Conservatives - but rather to attack the enemy within, in this case the moderates.

On each occasion the Left concentrated on strengthening its hold. At this first conference on 1 June, the left-oriented National Executive Committee sought endorsement of its policy statement, which included sweeping measures of nationalisation and the abolition of a second chamber of Parliament. Callaghan, though opposed to many of the measures, spoke in favour of an uncompromisingly socialist programme.

Moderates in the Party found this conference particularly depressing and the NEC's draft manifesto sterile and inward-looking to the point of chauvinism. If there had been any doubt in their minds previously, they were under no illusion now. Not only had the Right been refused any considered hearing, it had also been jeered. Owen, who according to one participant made "a brave speech", was booed. Some saw this incident as a personal turning point for David Owen. He had previously wished to have no truck with those thinking of defecting. He now became the toughest representative of the Right. At this stage he approached Bill Rodgers and Shirley Williams, suggesting they should jointly make the running.

At the same time as the Labour Party was showing its tough public face in Wembley, a rather subdued private face was emerging from at least one office inside the party. Peter Shore's special assistant, David Cowling, had prepared a private document for Shore assessing Labour's performance since May 1979 and indicating just how difficult the road to future electoral victory was going to be.

Labour had really failed to benefit from the unpopularity of the Tory government, and, according to Cowling, that was its only real electoral advantage.

The size of the problem was not generally appreciated. In 1979, Labour's share of votes cast was the lowest since 1931 (in actual fact, Labour's share was also higher in 1929 than in 1979).

To win the next general election was an awesome task. To win a parliamentary majority of even one seat would mean winning forty-nine extra seats, requiring a two-party swing of 3.7%. To achieve a reasonable and secure majority of forty seats would involve winning eighty-eight extra seats, which would require an unprecedented swing of 7.2%.

The author went further, highlighting the fact that constituency boundaries were to be re-drawn, presumably before the next elections - further exacerbating Labour's problem. The best unofficial Labour Party estimates indicated a loss through boundary changes of an additional fifteen to twenty seats, signalling a net advantage to the Conservatives of thirty to forty seats.

Labour's task was to attract an additional two million voters before the next election. A tall order, Cowling thought.

Nor did the analysis take into account a future social democrat party and the loss of voters that would follow. And as the Labour Pary seemed to move inexorably leftward, steam-rolling the moderates in its ranks, the lone voice from Brussels was heard again. This time, addressing the Parliamentary Press Club, Roy Jenkins likened the new party to a plane at the end of the runway, which could either crash in the field beyond, or soar into the sky. Again the speech prompted a huge response from people who welcomed the idea of a new grouping in British politics, confirming that somewhere out there, the troops were standing by. As before, there were left-wing opponents. To some, Jenkins was henceforth to be known simply as 'Biggles of Brussels' after the schoolboy adventure stories.

By the time of Jenkins's second major speech, 'the Group' was at the point of splitting. Certainly John Horam had been concerned that the Group was "too oriented on Roy Jenkins". A future party, he felt, needed to be more broadly based, and to him and half the Group the inclusion, at the very least, of Williams and Rodgers was crucial.

However, neither Shirley Williams nor indeed Bill Rodgers were always seen as totally unambiguous in their intention to leave Labour and start up in opposition. Clearly the decision to leave the Party, with which they had been associated for decades, was not going to be easy, particularly perhaps for Mrs Williams who had the reputation of being unable to make up her mind about matters in general, let alone about so crucial and irrevocable a step.

It was around this time that Shirley Williams said that there was no future for a centre party without roots. It was also then, following one of her speeches, that she received hundreds of letters urging her to stay inside the Labour party. Dick Taverne recalls an exchange of letters between them, when Shirley Williams accepted this view. Taverne had written to her that the matter was too important for sentiment, that she would not regain moderate right control of the Party, that the grassroots and the unions had now gone too far left, and that by remaining in the Labour Party she would make the adoption of policies she opposed more likely. That if she delayed her decision to leave, the only alternative for the electorate would be the Thatcher government. Says Taverne: "Shirley Williams wrote me a letter, stating she would continue to fight from within the Party, for the right sensible policies, under the leadership of Denis Healey."

However, Healey was a disappointment to those who looked to him either to regain moderate control of the Party or, when things appeared to have gone too far, to break away. Some Social Democrats think that Healey could have become the leader - he was in the right place to do so. He was in Parliament. Jenkins was in Brussels. But, they say, he was confidently waiting for Callaghan's mantle to fall over his own shoulders.

He misread the situation, for by the time Callaghan announced his retirement as leader, left-wing pressure had become so strong that this transformed whatever results might have occurred earlier. By the autumn it had become clear that future leadership elections would be decided by an electoral college. So the PLP decided to jump the gun - against the wishes and admonitions of diverse voices on the left - so that they could, for the last time, control the election. However, it was not Healey but Michael Foot who came out top.

Foot had already shown that he had considerable support within the PLP in the previous 1976 election when he had won on the first ballot. This time, although Healey led on the first ballot, Foot became leader. It was widely assumed that Foot had won the final necessary votes from centre Labour MPs who were anxious not to precipitate an early repeat of the election, which might, with the new, wider franchise, let in Benn. Many liked Foot personally and hoped that by choosing him they were settling the leadership issue for some years to come. To vote in Healey would inevitably have been the signal for new disputes between Right and Left, more "dirty washing in public", probably leading to a second leadership election within a year or so. Foot represented a good compromise solution: a man who satisfied the Left with his immaculate left-wing credentials but who was seen by the Right as a champion of parliamentary democracy, and who, as a minister in the 1974-79 government, had been seen to

138

function within the parliamentary system of the establishment.

Healey had got it wrong. The leadership did not pass to him when Jim Callaghan retired. Nor, indeed, was it long before even his deputy leadership was being disputed. Tony Benn was to mount a challenge within a matter of months, unpopular not only within the PLP but also amongst many of his traditional allies on the left of the Party. For by that time the SDP had been formed and much of the Left wished to stabilise the rocking boat.

Healey's earlier attitude is recalled by Social Democrats. He had sent messages to Brussels that Jenkins should not go it alone, that after Callaghan's retirement he, Healey would bring Labour back on course. Others remember him sitting at Conference listening to left-wing "juvenile rubbish", smiling broadly - literally and metaphorically sitting on his hands. Jim Daly recalls the visit of the CLV steering committee delegation when they came to the House of Commons to plead for more vigorous leadership for the Right of the Labour Party: "Healey got up and locked the door. He then treated us to lovely homilies how he and Callaghan could handle the situation. He was having talks with union bosses, in the old convention of fixing things, but he failed to understand the new reality."

Leadership from the Right was forthcoming, however, when David Owen, Bill Rodgers and Shirley Williams acted openly in concert for the first time. "We are not prepared to abandon Britain to divisive and often cruel Tory policies because electors do not have an opportunity to vote for an acceptable socialist alternative", ran the headline in the *Guardian* on 1 August 1980. This was the now famous open letter to their fellow members of the Labour Party. With this letter they nailed their colours to the mast. From now on they were to work more visibly toward the creation of "an acceptable socialist alternative", towards the launching of the Social Democratic Party.

The next day, the *Guardian* spontaneously referred to Owen, Rodgers and Williams as the 'Gang of Three'. The name was readily accepted by their enemies and also became an easy handle for press and public to identify the trio of dissenting politicians. The parallel to the Gang of Four - Mao Tse Tung's widow and her three associates who were being tried as enemies of China in the post-Mao regime - was inappropriate in all but this, being seen as the 'enemy within'. If the Chinese

Gang of Four were the extremist enemies of a moderate regime, the English Gang of Three were the very opposite, the moderate opponents of a less than moderate Party. Within a few months, the return of expatriate Roy Jenkins was to make possible the use of the Chinese designation in toto, the Gang of Three becoming the Gang of Four.

For the moment, though, it was the Gang of Three who pleaded openly with their comrades in the Labour Party, seeking to prevent a decisive and perhaps irreversible shift to the left at the conference in October. Their letter was in a sense the last attempt to forestall a final turn of the screw.

Had the letter done its job and steered the conference and the Party more toward the left centre, balancing left and right concepts within the party, would the Gang of Three have set up in business on their own? It is one of those fascinating questions to which future historians may wish to return. What is certain is that all three, and particularly at this point Williams and Rodgers, were well aware of the traumatic nature of the proposed break, and the practical electoral difficulties of creating a new alternative radical party. Had the Party been prepared to work toward sensible economic and international policies, and toward a party democracy involving the total membership rather than the "caucus", they might well have gone on fighting within Labour: "We have already said that we will not support a centre party for it would lack roots and a coherent philosophy." But the corollary to this followed: "If the Labour Party abandons its democratic and international principles, the argument may grow for a new democratic socialist party of conscience and reform committed to those principles."

Shortly afterwards, another appeal to the Labour Party found its way into the press, this time from twelve Labour MPs: Mike Thomas John Cartwright, Tom Ellis, Ian Wrigglesworth, John Roper and John Horam, who were to become first wave Social Democrat MPs; George Robertson, Alan Fitch, William Hamilton, Thomas Unwin, Arthur Palmer, who are still Labour MPs, and Eric Ogden who continues as Labour MP but was the first MP to be caught under the new re-selection procedure confirmed at the Blackpool Conference of October 1980. Led by Mike Thomas and nicknamed 'The Dirty Dozen', they were the joint signatories of a letter to *The Times* entitled: 'Why the Labour Party must change'. They stated simply that the left-dominated NEC was unrepresentative of the party as a whole, and that even if a balance between Right and Left could be voted in at the forthcoming conference, this would still leave the NEC unrepresentative of the party membership, which was more moderate. Labour policy statements were "unimaginative and doctrinaire in tone, pinning their hopes on the old formulae of public ownership, state intervention and moves towards protectionism and avoiding many of the real issues."

In addition, they said, the poor financial state of the party was giving the trade unions greater control over the party - an electoral disadvantage. Instead, they argued, it was time to loosen the ties between the unions and the Party, "to reform the relationship between the political and industrial wings of the Labour movement". The trade unions themselves were changing. On the one hand, those who even ten years ago considered affiliation to the Labour Party were now apparently not interested - the teachers, for example, and local government officers (though NALGO was to put it to a ballot of members within fifteen months or so). On the other hand, "with the phenomenal growth of white-collar unionism, a smaller and smaller proportion of trade union members are Labour supporters". The article continued: "In other unions the proportion of members paying the political levy is falling off", quoting Clive Jenkins' union, the Association of Scientific, Technical and Managerial Staffs, where 70% had opted out.

While the unions themselves "have been growing away from party political adherence, their continuing role as provider of finance and of block votes at the party conference may not be appropriate for a democratic socialist party in the 1980s and 1990s."

Equally inappropriate for a democratic socialist party, the signatories argued, were the proposed left-wing changes toward party democracy. While the signatories accepted that changes were due, they envisaged a much wider democracy. They argued strongly against entrusting democracy to unrepresentative groups of activists, sometimes accounting for one quarter of one percent or even less of Labour voters. Party members of say one year's standing should be involved in selection and re-selection of MPs. All Party members should be involved in the decision-making process. This would give greater democratic authority to the constituency parties, to their delegates to Conference, to the NEC, and to the manifesto.

Concern was expressed that the Blackpool conference in October 1980 might merely paper over the cracks in the party structure. In the event, they need not have feared. This was to be the end of fudging. John Horam, one of the 'Dirty Dozen', says retrospectively: "I thought we would win in Blackpool. I was surprised but actually not displeased. After years of Labour fudging, the issues were no longer being fudged. Now I knew where I stood. Since then every victory for the Left has been a victory for me."

Certainly, if the Left had been setting out to create a situation which was totally unacceptable to those on the right of the Party, they could scarcely have done a more thorough job. On issues of party democracy and of home and international policy, Conference voted against the fundamental beliefs of the moderates. To add insult to injury, the Right's expectation of improving their showing on the NEC was squashed: instead of gaining two voices, they actually lost one, with the new balance of eighteen to eleven against them.

So when the *Economist* drew its conclusion that the Labour Party had moved nearer to a split than at any time in its history, it was nearer the mark than James Callaghan, who optimistically referred to the centre party as "dead as a dodö.

For the moment, Conference had said' yes' to immediate withdrawal from the Common Market, without commitment to the referendum advocated by David Owen. Previously that one issue alone had been important enough for Shirley Williams to have threatened possible withdrawal from the Party. The conference had said 'yes' to unilateral nuclear disarmament, though 'no' to quitting NATO - a decision harking back to the Gaitskell era of defeat and subsequent fight-back. The Conference said 'yes' to more nationalisation and to the speedy dispatch of the House of Lords.

It also agreed to an electoral college for electing the party leader, though the composition of the college was not yet decided. That was to be debated and settled separately, at the third conference within eight months, in January 1981. The conference voted for compulsory re-selection of parliamentary candidates between elections but rejected, by the slimmest of margins, the proposal that the NEC should have control over the Party's election manifesto. No-one doubted that the Left, having won through on MP re-selection and leadership elections, would return to fight another day on the manifesto issue.

142

Most newspapers, committed Left excepted, commented with one voice upon this conference. So while a *Tribune* article referred to Shirley Williams showing the "ugly face of moderation" (3 October 1980), and while the opposition were wont to refer to the Campaign for Labour Victory as the Campaign for luncheon vouchers, the large circulation papers of right and left described the week's events with stark and depressing words.

The *Sunday Times*: "... the squabbles threw up, and it is the correct verb, a package of policies almost by accident, which, if they were ever to be enacted, would be a big step on the road to serfdom and to destitution ... The conference was above all a defeat for millions of ordinary Labour supporters who prefer moderation but are not properly represented among the militant cliques and caucuses... Many must have been revolted by the rampant class hatred."

The *Guardian* (Peter Jenkins, 4 October 1980): "My nightmare of this week is that political liberty is now at threat in Britain, for I cannot feel confident that it would long survive the coming to power of the people who have taken hold of the Labour Party ... Not many of the lay delegates who spoke this week seemed to be speaking out of working-class experience; more often they mouthed the jargon of paperback Marxism. The participatory revolt which has rocked the Labour movement is the revolt of the lumpen polytechnic ... Just about everything the 'Gang of Three' warned of in their open letter has come to pass. Their three tests of a viable democratic socialist party - its commitments to a mixed economy, to internationalism and to representative democracy - were failed at Blackpool this week. All of us who hold those values are nearer to the end of the road."

The *Observer* (5 October 1980): "The Party is so riven by internal dissension that it is no longer an effective opposition...that is bad not only for the Party but for our democracy."

The Times: "... behind all the Blackpool farce looms a tragedy that compels seriousness touched with near despair."

And in the *Daily Mail* (3 October 1980): 'The Dream that died at Blackpool', which commented as follows: "A new political party came into being ... It has assumed to itself the name of the once great party it replaced. ... I refer, of course, to the Labour Party, the old and the new. The old Labour Party, the party of Attlee, Gaitskell, Wilson and Callaghan, has gone. It gave only the merest whimper of protest as it took its last

143

shuddering gasp and expired forever.

"The new Labour Party is a cat of a different breed altogether. It is made up of hard-faced fanatics, intolerant hucksters of a political tradition alien to everything for which this country stands, people who speak pejoratively of 'parliamentarianism' and who say 'We can't afford the luxury of conscience ... conscience is a cop-out.'" The article advocates that a Healey-led Parliamentary Labour Party should go solo, split from the rest of the Labour movement through a kind of Unilateral Declaration of Independence. It foresees two Labour Parties emerging: "But can anyone really doubt that of a Parliamentary Labour Party led by Denis Healey, and a Labour Party led by Tony Benn it would be the parliamentary party which would win?"

This proposal must always have counted as one of the more fanciful and is now relegated to the dusty archives of the *Daily Mail*. But the article is entirely at one with the other mass media in its basic attitude of grave disquiet at Labour's leftward lurch.

For Callaghan the conference was a personal disaster. He had believed that he, Jim, could once again fix it. No need to reform the NEC - a bit of bargaining here, a bit of horse-trading there, and mandatory re-selection would not go through. Neither would NEC control the manifesto, and he would be able to achieve a compromise over the leadership election procedure by accepting an electoral college, but with the PLP getting the lion's share of the votes. In the event, Callaghan lost out on re-selection, and on the leadership election - which was finally to give the PLP a mere 30% of the votes; he just scraped home on the manifesto by a slim margin of votes, for the moment ensuring joint NEC-PLP control. Callaghan's staunch arguments against nuclear disarmament were to no avail. The Common Market he ignored. The overall drive for party unity was doomed to failure. Said Frank Chapple, General Secretary of the Electrical, Electronic, Telecommunication and Plumbing Union: "It is his compromises which have got us into this position. His pleas for unity are simply surrenders to the Left. Mr Callaghan should resign at once." (*Observer* 5 October 1980).

While Callaghan's reputation suffered sadly at the 1980 annual conference - and he was to resign the following month - the Gang of Three proved themselves leaders for their cause. In Shirley Williams' words: "for evil to triumph, it is necessary only that good men do nothing." She and Rodgers and Owen were now doers. She gave one of the memorable speeches at one of two excellently attended CLV meetings. She also improved her own vote count on the NEC from 4,774,000 to 5,244,000 votes, an extraordinary achievement in the circumstances.

On the first day of the conference, at a packed meeting organised by the Campaign for Labour Victory, Shirley Williams rallied the moderates within Labour. Symbolically this was on the twentieth anniversary of Gaitskell's famous 'fight and fight and fight again' speech and her words had a Gaitskell ring about them: "The time has come when you had better stick your heads up over the parapet and start fighting ... because if you don't there will not be a Labour Party worth the name." She went on: "We are going to fight to save this Party and by God I think we can."

But twenty years on from Gaitskell's speech, developments were to happen faster and turn out differently. Where Gaitskell's defeat inside the Party had been reversed within one year, this time, within six months, Shirley Williams and her colleagues had gone up and over the parapet.

As for Roy Jenkins, in spite of the backing and prompting of enthusiastic supporters such as Colin Phipps, Michael Barnes and SDA's Stephen Haseler and Douglas Eden, the summer had, according to political friends, been his low point. Increasingly he had been feeling that, although the idea of a new grouping in the Left Centre of British politics was sound, it was premature. He felt the lack of a coherent social democratic philosophy to meet the well-delineated challenge of both the Thatcher government and the Bennite Socialists, and believed that intellectual application was required before taking decisive steps. He also began to think, like other observers, that the October conference would be a partial victory for the Right within Labour, and thus once again fudge the issues.

At least on the second count, he need not have worried. The Labour Party conference was tailor-made for someone waiting in the wings; it gave the greatest possible encouragement to waverers to seek sanctuary in an alternative party of the left.

Jenkins, having hesitated over the summer, clearly took heart from the clarity of the outcome of the Blackpool conference and made plans to re-enter British politics. In Brussels he let it be known that after 6 January 1981, when his term of office as President of the European Commission came to an end, he would be making a series of speeches which would set out a middle way in economic policy.

With Rodgers saying in a radio interview: "This Labour Party is not fit to form a government", and Owen, in Wales, making it clear that an electoral college was only acceptable on a one-Party-member-one-vote basis, the countdown to the Special Party Conference on 24 January 1981 had started. It was evident from the political drift, however, that this system could not materialise. The exact breakdown of votes was still to be decided, but the one-member-one-vote idea had no realistic chance.

So, when the CLV held a further conference, six months after their May meeting in Birmingham, the atmosphere was quite changed. Participants were for the first time openly talking of leaving the Party. Previously those who had spoken of leaving had been regarded as revolutionary or treacherous by others there. This time, many speakers referred to the 'end of the road'. Before, David Owen had been the coolest about breaking from the Party. Now he was the most hawkish - a remarkable transformation within six months. The electoral college would be the test. "We cannot", said Owen, "participate in a fraudulent electoral system ... To those of you who think it's time to go, I say this, we are going to have a Socialist Party, a genuine SDP seen to be on the left, with strong links with the trade unions, but before you do it, you have to be seen to have exhausted all the real possibilities. It has to be the kind of party that we can all join. Let's jump our fences one by one, but Beechers Brook is on January 24."

This conference was held on 25 October 1980 at Frank Chapple's EEPTU Centre in Highbury, under the auspices of the Campaign for Labour Victory. It could have been more appropriately called the Campaign for Labour Defeat. Or to quote the words of one grassroots delegate from Leicester: "It has been said that we must be a party inside a party but maybe we must face the fact that after January 24 what is needed is a party outside the party."

Now in the autumn the new party was virtually under way. Offices were found in Queen Anne's Gate. The move there took place within a week of the Council for Social Democracy being declared. The Gang of Three gave speeches to rally opinion for electing Labour leaders on a one-member-one-vote basis but this was, to quote Owen's words, chiefly a question of being "seen to have exhausted all real possibilities".

Williams and Rodgers were still uneasy and undecided.

Those around them were unsure: "Nobody knew whether the three would jump". Dick Taverne remembers that Bill Rodgers at this stage was the most reluctant to leave, unsure whether enough Labour MPs would follow. "He was also refusing to see me", a sign that he, Rodgers, was not prepared to be seen to burn his bridges.

The Gang of Three went over to Brussels and talked to Jenkins. But it was Owen, in December, who took a decision first. "In maximum security" he held a series of meetings with those Labour MPs who were prime candidates for a new party. He also talked to others to take soundings, but he made it clear that Jenkins alone was not the basis for a new party. He, Owen would be leaving, but the key to the new party was Shirley Williams, who by now had informed her constituency that she would not be standing there again for Labour.

Amidst this uncertainty, Jenkins' imminent return, set for 6 January, loomed. His close supporters were concerned that the home-coming should not turn out to be a terrible anti-climax. They felt he had to come back to something and toyed with the idea of creating an Institute of Policy Research as a kind of neutral political platform. Over lunch at Clive Lindley's home in the first week of January, with the Brussels job behind him, Jenkins met David Marquand, Dick Taverne, Matthew Oakeshott, Lord Harris, and Jim Daly. Lindley says: "We had an exciting meeting. We decided that whether the Gang of Three made their move or not, we would make ours by March."

When Jenkins returned to England, according to Dick Taverne: "He found the Gang of Three in total disarray. Owen was the toughest and wanted to make the break immediately. Shirley Williams did not want to go till after the local elections in May. And Bill Rodgers by now didn't want to go at all. It was Jenkins who brought them all together. He persuaded them to sign the Limehouse Declaration which he himself had largely drafted."

The Wembley Conference had decided that the electoral college should comprise trade unions with 40% of the vote, constituency parties with 30%, and the Parliamentary Labour Party with 30%. The one-member-one-vote idea was dead. Social Democracy had been born.

PART V

THE SHOW ON THE ROAD

Chapter Seventeen

LIMEHOUSE TO WARRINGTON

On 26 January 1981, the Gang of Four issued the following declaration, to be known subsequently as the Limehouse Declaration:

"The calamitous outcome of the Labour Party Wembley conference demands a new start in British politics. A handful of trade union leaders can now dictate the choice of a future Prime Minister.

"The conference disaster is the culmination of a long process by which the party has moved steadily away from its roots in the people of this country and its commitment to parliamentary government.

"We propose to set up a Council for Social Democracy. Our intention is to rally all those who are committed to the values, principles and policies of Social Democracy.

"We seek to reverse Britain's economic decline. We want to create an open, classless and more equal society, one which rejects ugly prejudices based on sex, race or religion.

"A first list of those who have agreed to support the council will be announced at an early date. Some of them have been actively and continuously engaged in Labour politics. A few were so engaged in the past but have ceased to be so recently. Others have been mainly active in spheres outside party politics.

"We do not believe the fight for the ideals we share and for the recovery of our country should be limited only to politicians. It will need the support of men and women in all parts of our society.

"The Council will represent a coming together of several streams: politicians who recognise that the drift towards extremism in the Labour Party is not compatible with the democratic traditions of the party they joined, and those from outside politics who believe that the country cannot be saved without changing the sterile and rigid framework into which the British political system has increasingly fallen in the past

151

two decades.

"We do not believe in the politics of an inert centre merely representing the lowest common denominator between two extremes. We want more, not less, radical change in our society but with a greater sense of direction.

"Our economy needs a healthy public sector and a healthy private sector without frequent frontier changes. We want to eliminate poverty and promote greater equality without stifling enterprise or imposing bureaucracy from the centre. We need the innovating strength of a competitive economy with a fair distribution of rewards.

"We favour competitive public enterprise, co-operative ventures and profit-sharing. There must be more decentralisation of decision-making in industry and government, together with an effective and practical system of democracy at work.

"The quality of our public and community services must be improved and they must be made more responsive to people's needs.

"We do not accept that mass unemployment is inevitable. A number of countries, mainly those with Social Democratic governments, have managed to combine high employment with low inflation.

"Britain needs to recover its self-confidence and be outward looking, rather than isolationist, xenophobic or neutralist. We want Britain to play a full and constructive role within the framework of the European Community, NATO, the United Nations and the Commonwealth.

"It is only within such a multilateral framework that we can hope to negotiate international agreements covering arms control and disarmament, and to grapple effectively with the poverty of the Third World.

"We recognise that for those people who have given much of their lives to the Labour Party the choice that lies ahead will be deeply painful. But we believe that the need for a re-alignment of British politics must now be faced."

With the issuing of the Limehouse Declaration, events moved at an astonishing speed. For that simple declaration prompted a response which surprised everybody, from the Gang of Four themselves to media commentators and to opposition parties. No-one could have predicted then that, by the end of the year, the Social Democrats in alliance with the Liberals would be hot favourites to form a government at the next general election.

Within five weeks, on 2 March, the Four gave notice that the Council for Social Democracy would be translated into a new political party before Easter. From that day on, the first MPs sat in the House as Social Democrats. A dozen former Labour MPs, including Bill Rodgers and David Owen, resigned from the Party, resigned the Labour Party Whip, as did nine Labour Lords in the House of Lords. This action so soon after the Limehouse Declaration followed from evidence of considerable support in the country: "We have received over 25,000 messages of support which express an overwhelming desire to be given the opportunity to vote at the next election for social democrats."

All was set for the launch of the new party on 26 March 1981. And what a launch it was, self-conscious in the glare of publicity. A full eighty-one years separated this from the last launch of a major new party, but the gap could figuratively have been measured in light-years. For when the Labour Party's forerunner, the Labour Representation Committee, was created on 27 and 28 February 1900 it was not even clear whether its aim was to be a party at all. A short, sober article in *The Times* merely gave a factual account of the business conducted over the two days.

The Times heading then of 'Labour Representation in Parliament' could scarcely compete with the newspaper's brasher announcement eighty-one years later: 'The Gang becomes a Party'. In 1900, the launch of the Labour Party, an item of limited interest in a world dominated by the Boer War, was dismissed in a few editorial inches.

The Social Democratic Party, employing experts, organised a highly professional, american-style razzamatazz of a day with press conferences in London and major provincial cities. It was an occasion when politicians and journalists together created history and revelled in it, flying together in chartered aeroplanes. However earnest they all were about the significance of the occasion, this day was mainly notable for its glitter. Politics and policies was for later. For the moment the serious (and not so serious) newspapers ran the story with headlines like 'Shirley on the Treadmill' (*Observer*), 'Williams enjoys day out with media' (*Guardian*), 'Maiden flight of a Social Democrat' (*The Sunday Telegraph*). About five hundred journalists and twenty-five or so TV crews were at the press conference in London.

At 8.45, at the Connaught Rooms in London, came opening statements and questions. The Gang of Four then caught planes and trains for follow-up press conferences in the provinces. The new party, preaching decentralisation, was putting its money where its mouth was: there was more to Britain than London, a theme to be echoed in the autumn when the SDP held its first split-site national conference, not at the seaside, like the other parties, but in Perth, Bradford and London.

For the moment, the logistics of launching the party were formidable: press conferences in ten cities on one day. After their morning conference in London, the Four separated and between 13.00 and 14.00 hours, Williams in Edinburgh, Rodgers in Norwich, Jenkins in Cardiff, and Owen in Southampton held their next sessions with the media. By the evening they had chaired press conferences in Birmingham, Leeds, Manchester and Plymouth. In Aberdeen, the second Scottish conference of the day was presided over by a former junior Labour minister, Bob Maclennan.

The media responded, recognising a good story when they saw one. The *Financial Times* wrote: "Mrs Shirley Williams had given seven television interviews, at least a dozen radio interviews... and had left a trail of niceness across 700 miles of Britain" and also reported: "A girl stood outside the door of the room where Mrs Williams was giving interviews with a watch in her hand. At three-minute intervals she called 'Time up' and the next group was wheeled in like a team in a relay race." The Lobby Correspondent of the *Financial Times* added: "At every point she was photographed. Even her lunch, an appropriately wholesome sandwich made with wholemeal bread, was recorded for posterity." To round it all off, an artist armed with easel and brush was there to record, in his own words, 'this historic occasion'.

At each of the conference centres, 'phone banks' were manned by the SDP ready to answer the public's questions. One of the functions of the phone banks was to proselytise, to sell the party to new members.

The publicity value of press and TV reports measured in cost per column inches was incalculable. Over the following months, editorial coverage was to continue in an extraordinary way. The media both reflected the public's intrinsic interest in a party which had clearly struck a chord in the land and helped by its coverage to create yet more interest. Early opinon polls, showing substantial support for the SDP and in particular for a possible SDP/Liberal alliance, were the foundation of the media's interest, but the SDP's growing popularity was undoubtably fed by the media's devoted interest.

Though the opposition's jibes about a media-created party were many, and though the party's meteoric rise is evident enough, it is easy to forget that all was not plain sailing at first. Real doubts existed in those early months as to the ultimate survival of the Social Democratic Party.

The period from Limehouse to Warrington was characterised as much by question marks about the future as by manifestations of success. Political commentators trod cautiously when forecasting the new centre grouping's breakthrough into the mainstream of British politics. No new party had emerged successfully in eighty years. It could all still crumble. Meteors fade. And the greatest danger for the Social Democrats was any sign of failure. Just as success breeds success, so failure could be self-perpetuating. It was not till Warrington that the picture became really clear. Warrington was the watershed: the party's inability to capture the seat did not prevent this from being its greatest triumph (see next chapter). From that moment on, the Social Democratic Party's success was unambiguous and ever more clear.

Until the Warrington by-election the fear of failure haunted the party. There was furthermore a distinct slackening in the bandwagon's speed. In May/June 1981, the SDP was threatened by a kind of paralysis, for every decision could bring failure and decline. But lack of decisions was no recipe for success either. As the heady launch gave way to the morning after, May and June opinion polls began to show some slackening in support: on 14 May the *Daily Telegraph* reported the latest Gallup findings under the heading 'SDP support falls as the limelight fades'. A month later, on 14 June, the *Sunday Times*, reporting MORI findings, wrote "One in three of the voters who plumped for the Social Democrats when the party was launched in March now have deserted them."

Little wonder that Social Democrats were running scared. Since they could not risk failure, as Hugo Young put it in the *Sunday Times* of 31 May 1981, "the most conscious decision it (the SDP leadership) appears to have taken is to postpone most of the important choices". Policies could not be decided; neither could the leadership question be resolved until the party's constitution had been agreed. In a new party claiming to be devoted to the principle of democracy, the involvement of its membership in the decision-making process was imperative, and yet this principle could not be put into practice until a constitution had been formally adopted. Still, the party chose to defer the drawing-up of its constitution till February 1982.

With no legal reality to prop it up, with no single leader, with no agreed policies, and with opinion poll ratings sliding, the SDP was in a no-man's land between runaway success and possible eclipse. Although it needed to prove itself in the only way that counted, i.e. in the polling booths, it was loth to take the risk.

The first by-election which the SDP could fight was in Warrington, one of the toughest to contest. Humiliation here might have ended the Social Democratic dream, hence the hesitations and the 'dithering', as the media unsympathetically called it.

Similar caution was demonstrated in the refusal of the Social Democrat MP defectors to gamble their seats, the subject of considerable criticism at the time. Labour MPs crossed the floor of the House, at the outset and throughout the year, without submitting themselves to the test of re-election. Not that this was in any way improper. Precedents included Winston Churchill. But the argument that a man elected under one party's label has no moral authority to continue to represent his constituency if he switches party, does have some validity, and understandably the Labour Party made political capital of this. The counter-arguments with which the SDP justified the retention of seats by their MPs were somewhat thin; the Party had struck a balance between ideal morality and political caution.

In 1973 Dick Taverne had created a precedent. He had resigned his Labour seat in Lincoln and fought on an independent ticket, a gamble which had come off magnificently. In 1981, the first Labour politician to resign and fight a by-election under a Social Democrat label was Anne Sofer. Mrs Sofer had been elected in the May Council elections as Labour Councillor of the Greater London Council. In November she not only switched to the SDP (the first GLC councillor to do so) but re-presented herself as an SDP candidate in a by-election. She did this on her own initiative and she won. It was an important psychological breakthrough: the first SDP gain following on from resignation. The SDP, though strengthened by Mrs Sofer's convincing win, still did not deviate from its policy of caution. However by now, in the autumn of 1981, Labour and Conservative parties were equally anxious not to be compelled to go to the polls by forcing unnecessary by-elections.

But in early summer perhaps the most visible loss of SDP momentum came with the May council elections. It was these elections which, before the creation of the SDP, had made Mrs Williams hesitate about the timing of the party's launch. She had been of the opinion that this should be delayed until they were safely out of the way since the new party would not be properly prepared to do battle. Though the party was launched in March, the SDP followed the path of discretion as the better part of valour and opted out of the council elections. The only Social Democrats running were unofficial and not backed by the SDP.

So the SDP sat out the elections in May, a period coinciding with the party's drop in popularity. On the night of the election results, Shirley Williams seemed literally to be sitting it out, as TV viewers saw her commenting on results which concerned neither her directly nor the SDP. Somehow, that evening, a tired and unconvincing Shirley Williams speaking from the sidelines of politics, herself at that point an ex-MP only, signalled a low in the party's fortunes. Though the Liberals made good gains and some unofficial Social Democrats did quite well, this was still a moment of two-party control of the country. As the Conservatives lost ground, it was Labour who picked up the pieces, regaining control of fifteen counties lost in 1977.

If the fortunes of the new party then hung in the balance, it was not so for long. The Conservative and Labour parties continued to conspire, or so it seemed, to ensure the successful progress of the new Social Democratic Party. Whatever lack of positive SDP initiatives there might have been, they were more than offset by the Government's unsuccessful economic performance and by the Labour Party's intensification of its own civil war. Two years on from the propulsion of Mrs Thatcher into power, the Conservative Government was more unpopular than ever before. The electorate, informed that the main plank of the Government's economic policy was reduction of inflation, saw on the contrary an increase in inflation, as well as a dramatic rise in unemployment. Mrs Thatcher's uncompromising style of leadership merely augmented the electorate's hostility and/or disillusion. In spite of some Conservative voices in the background pleading for greater flexibility in the face of human hardship, in spite of 364 university economists urging a U-turn in policy, the Conservative machine steamrollered on.

However, it was the Labour Party which seemed bent on its suicide mission, with a collective finger on the self-destruct button. To an outside observer the actions of the Labour Party were scarcely credible. Every move seemed designed to hasten the process of disintegration, to ensure that whatever the SDP's failings, they would be insignificant beside Labour's convulsions. To lifelong supporters of the great Party, the ever-increasing and destructive hostilities were little short of tragic. Labour seemed destined to shed much of its support and ensure that the infant SDP grew strong.

The splits in the Labour Party became more serious, and more numerous. Four main factions could be pinpointed. First, the social democrats still inside the Labour Party who might be tempted to follow the first batch. Second, those of the Right who intended to fight from inside - men like Mellish, Healey and Hattersley. Third and fourth, the Left split down the middle, with the Bennite Left, or hard or looney Left on one side and the soft or sensible Left, identified with people like Neil Kinnock and Joan Lestor on the other. The Tribune Group split. That part of the Tribune Group represented by Kinnock, Lestor and Michael Foot effectively became the new centre around which those seeking party unity sought to regroup.

At this point one should look at the leader's role in the continuing saga of the Labour Party. Michael Foot took over in November 1980, as a compromise candidate with the best chance of holding the Party together. But it was too late. By then the Party was on the point of disintegration. Michael Foot inherited the task of an Admiral Dönitz after Hitler, or at any rate of an Emperor Charles after Franz Joseph in the Austro-Hungarian Empire of 1916. By then the die was cast.

It is difficult to conceive how any alternative leader might have succeeded where Foot has failed. He has been criticised often enough for his weakness, his inability to act; he has been criticised by both the Left and the Right; he has been criticised by the public at large. Would even Wilson, the past-master have fared better?

Foot, at the end of his career, having made his reputation during decades of political campaigning as a passionate champion of Left wing causes, now found himself trying to bridge the gap between the irreconcilable positions: unity at all costs, to stop defections to the SDP; unity between Conference and Shadow Cabinet to consolidate on one parcel of policies; unity across the Party. In the search for accommodation, Michael Foot was ready to sacrifice, or at least adapt, his own left-wing stance: on unilateralism and on the question of witch-hunts of the extreme Left. For Foot, the immediate priority was to consolidate and prepare for the general elections.

But Foot, as any Labour leader at this stage, was bound to fail. And if there was one man who would make absolutely sure of such a failure, it was Tony Benn. Just as the Social Democratic contingent no longer aspired to a unified Labour Party, so Benn rejected party unity. By now the extreme Left and Right of the party were united on at least one point - that unity in the wrong cause was not worth having. Foot's every move to consolidate and to hold out olive branches was therefore doomed to fail; every healing gesture was countered by yet another wounding blow.

Benn's role in the continuing saga of the Left's intensifying struggle for control over the party was crucial. Around him, Labour's extreme Left, both democratic and undemocratic, could crystallise. Benn undoubtedly provided leadership and a vision which galvanised the uncompromising Left to a campaign unremittingly fought toward their goal: the pre-eminence of Party. The vision of that party's power might have differed according to the factions among Benn's followers, whether democratic or undemocratic, but the model ahead, sooner or later, was the East European model. For Benn's opponents, the 'leading role of the Party', as practised in Communist Europe, was an unacceptable prospect for the Labour Party, to be resisted at all costs.

A new dividing line inside Labour now came into being. No longer primarily between right and left, the new groupings were broadly 'unity first' against 'uncompromising Left'.

The 'unity first' group was an amalgamation of factions of the old style Labour Party, the old Broad Church concept re-appearing to save the disintegrating Party: a coalition of interests from the Labour Right through the Centre to what might be termed the old-fashioned Tribune Left, now becoming known as the Soft Left. This group emerged in February 1981 as the Labour Solidarity Campaign, or Solidarity for short - after Limehouse, but not in time to prevent the birth of the SDP.

Solidarity had little in common with the independent Polish Trade Union whose name it took. However, in its own way, Labour Solidarity was attempting to hold back the concept of a totalitarian party, albeit its own. Launched by one hundred MPs, Solidarity had as its chairmen Roy Hattersley and Peter Shore, and counted among its members Tribunites Arthur Davidson, Frank Field, Martin O'Neil and Joe Ashton.

Solidarity sought to provide a new political will to create a unified and vigorous Labour Party. It sought to show members of the Council for Social Democracy and would-be defectors that the Labour way was still open. Many of its aims were those of the Social Democrats: for parliamentary democracy, reversing the recent Wembley decision allotting Labour MPs a minority role in the election of party leaders; for a broadening of party democracy, ensuring the right of minority views to be respected. At the same time, Michael Foot appealed to would be defectors "even at this twelfth hour" not to go, for "those who leave us will become lonely figures in the political wilderness ... Their influence on events will be virtually nil."

But even as Solidarity and Michael Foot were trying to keep Social Democrats in, Tony Benn was doing his best to force them out. By seeking a commitment of loyalty to the Labour Party, he was attempting to make the Gang of Four's situation impossible. Although it can certainly be argued that Benn's call for an oath of loyalty was not unreasonable, its intention was to force splits, not to heal them.

Shirley Williams, as *The Times* reported on 29 January 1981, "took particular exception to the fact that she was being subjected to an inquisition about the activities of the social democratic group. While the Militant Tendency, the extreme left-wing group, was permitted to operate as a party within a party she did not see that anyone had any right to ask her any questions at all."

Indeed within less than a fortnight the first full-time Militant Tendency worker, Terry Harrison, was selected to stand as Labour candidate in Liverpool Edge Hill, a seat held by Liberal, David Alton. While Lord Underhill reacted by saying that: "The pattern in Liverpool is exactly what I warned of in my report which the National Executive refused to take up", David Alton was describing Harrison's views as making "Karl Marx look like a moderate."

It was not till the end of 1981 that the question of the Militant Tendency was to be taken in earnest, not by Benn who was campaigning for their right to be in the Labour Party, but by Foot. At that stage, Foot finally set the ball rolling for an investigation of the Militant Tendency's activities, a move which Bennites described as a witch hunt.

If Benn was taking it upon himself to lead the hard left-wing forces, he was developing some bitter enemies on the left of the party spectrum. Though he aroused extraordinary support in the constituency parties, as an orator, a man of charm and a disseminator of pure socialism, those who had closer knowledge saw him quite differently. Above all, they saw him as Tony-come-lately, a man converted rather later than many to the left-wing view, who was jumping on their bandwagon and taking it over for his own good as much as for the good of the left-wing ideas he purported to represent, indeed, to the detriment of those ideas. Benn's insistence on fighting for the deputy leadership of the Labour Party was considered inopportune and damaging to Labour and to the Left: once again the Labour Party would be diverted from the fight against the Tory government and the economic decline of the country by internal strife.

Tony Benn declared his candidacy at 3.30 in the morning of 3 April, at a time when the subject of the deputy leadership was about to be discussed by the Tribune Group, of which Benn had just become member. This also followed a personal appeal by Michael Foot, asking him, in the interests of party unity, not to stand.

Benn had jumped the gun. His Tribune colleagues had good reason to feel that he had played his own game at the expense of their collective interests. "One outcome", wrote the *New Statesman* (12 June 1981), "has been the deepest rift within the Tribune Group that its members can recall ... In part, Benn's opponents are making a tactical judgment: he is fighting the wrong battle at the wrong time. According to Judith Hart, 'his candidacy is jeopardising the political gains that the Left have made.'

Without doubt, Benn's decision to enter the contest against Denis Healey was of immense help to the brand new Social Democratic Party. Benn had thrown his cap into the ring within a week of the party's birth. For virtually six months the deputy leadership contest was to ensure that Labour partisans sniped at one another bitterly and ceaselessly. As Labour's reputation continued to sink, so the SDP's attractions inevitably grew as a party which provided a possible alternative.

Benn's campaign and above all Benn himself were tireless. In the light of new rules for electing leaders and deputy leaders, Benn went in particular for the important trade union votes, accounting for 40% of the votes to be cast. Soon it became evident that the contest would be close-run. Although the left wing had put up an alternative candidate, John Silkin, running on a party unity ticket, the contest always did look like a two-horse affair. The *Guardian* (3 April 1981), describing the two horses, had this to say: "Mr Healey is unlikely to fight the battle under Queensberry rules. And Mr Benn, though impeccable in his good manners and his disavowals of personality-politics, is supported by people who are considerably less fastidious about their tactics."

This was the era of the 'hit list', when the Bennite Left was preparing indexes of MPs who, by its own criteria, did not pass the test of socialism. The Rank and File Mobilising Committee, for example, published, as a service to its readers, 150 names (i.e. over half the Parliamentary Labour Party) of those who had signed a statement demanding that the new electoral college for voting in the Labour Party should be changed. This 'service' was generally regarded as a 'hit list'.

The Campaign for Labour Party Democracy published its own guide lines to help constituencies select the right person under the new re-selection procedures. It urged constituencies to refer to Hansard and check their MP's voting record, giving dates of ten crucial tests under Labour and Tory administrations. To satisfy these criteria MPs needed to prove, for example, that they had voted against their own Labour government on the 6 pay policy and on economic policies following the IMF loan.

Roy Hattersley, alluding to both the Rank and File Mobilising Committee and the Campaign for Labour Party Democracy, said: "I have genuinely no doubt that Tony Benn does not support many of the things that are done in his name. But it is essential for him to say so. I call upon him now to condemn all forms of intimidation within our party." Hattersley denounced the hit list of 150 MPs.

In the meantime, the new re-selection procedures were being implemented and the first right-wing casualties followed: Eric Ogden in Liverpool and John Sever in Birmingham failed to be re-selected. But the big debate of the time was the Left's attempt to tighten the rules under which re-selection took place. Not only had it now been agreed that re-selection was mandatory, regardless of whether a constituency party was happy with its MP or not, but the Left was also insisting that the constituency party was bound to offer competing names: the short list of one, of the sitting MP only, was not acceptable to the Campaign for Labour Party Democracy, or indeed to the left-wing NEC.

The aim of the hard Left was to flush out of the watered-down right-wing PLP as many of the Right as possible. In the event, the re-selection process, though throwing up close fights, shifted few sitting members in 1981. It did make MPs more careful not to flout carelessly the wishes of their largely leftist constituency parties. Hit lists and sheer hostility were powerful influences. In the meantime, many of the soft left Tribunites campaigned with the Right for CLPs' freedom to re-select their MP without competing candidates, citing bogus short lists. Neil Kinnock wrote to the *Guardian* (8 June 1981): "If it is not what a CLP wants, it is an affectation which can only result either in contrived contests that irritate and distract everyone concerned, or a pantomine democracy that invites ridicule." When Benn was re-selected it was just such a pantomime, a contrived contest against candidates only of the left who were not seeking to win but only going through the motions.

Whatever the rights and wrongs of the arguments within Labour, the electorate was never allowed to forget that the Labour Party was unable to run its own show, never mind the country. The infighting filled TV screens and the correspondence columns of the papers. The enemy within was attacked in endless hostile speeches in ever-more intemperate language, while no more than lip-service was paid to the fight against the Conservative Government, the real enemy. To Peter Shore, Shadow Chancellor and Co-chairman of Solidarity, Tony Benn was "the cuckoo in the nest", and Bennite politics were "the politics of paranoia".

On 3 June, Michael Foot took the unprecedented step of throwing down the gauntlet to Tony Benn: the issue was the Shadow Cabinet's commitment to Conference policies. The implication of Benn's campaign was that he, Benn, was the man to promote those policies, which Foot chose to interpret as a swipe not only at Healey, the sitting Deputy Leader, but at himself, the Leader too.

"I have told Tony Benn that, in my judgment, his only honest course now is to stand against me in the coming election for the leadership of the party." In a 2,500 word statement to the Shadow Cabinet, Foot went on: "It is clear that what he is challenging is the good faith of the Shadow Cabinet in carrying out its duties under the Labour Party Constitution. That is, above all and directly, an attack on my good faith." But, said Benn, a few hours after listening to Foot, in an interview on *Radio 4*, referring to Benn's 'politics of the kindergarten', "There is no question of my standing against him."

As the Benn campaign continued, another Bennite was making headlines. In May the electors of Greater London had voted in a Labour administration. The Labour take-over of London had been convincing though not overwhelming. Within sixteen hours of victory, the Labour moderate who had led his party to victory was ousted. Andrew McIntosh was replaced by Ken Livingstone. For the first time London was to be run by an administration of the far Left. Though Livingstone's take-over had been widely expected and democratically brought about, Londoners found themselves with a totally different team of people from those for whom they had voted. From then on, Londoners were treated to Livingstone's endless activity and pronouncements on matters concerning and not concerning London, about Northern Ireland and about gays, about reduction of bus fares (later to become more controversial than anticipated) and about unemployment. The spirit, though not the practice, of revolution was in the air.

Livingstone's new administration, faithful to its own style, chose not to accept any invitations to the Royal Wedding. What was perhaps more symptomatic of the state of the Labour Party was that so many on the left and on the right of the Party, like Roy Hattersley, also turned down their invitations, or were too busy on the day with matters of greater moment: the Deptford CLP fixed its re-selection meeting for that day, and John Silkin, its MP and contender for the deputy leadership, cried off because of a "previous engagement".

Though the Royal Wedding was not itself a matter of great import to the party, Labour's attitude was caused by internal strains, with each side feeling obliged to prove its socialist credentials. Meanwhile the electorate, uninhibited by dogma, openly showed its delight with both the spectacle and the fairy-tale quality of the wedding. It was one of those rare occasions when the country was united and happy, a festive occasion akin to a family celebration. The Royal Wedding seemed yet another sign that the Labour Party was out of step with the public, the electorate.

July, the month of the wedding, was also the month of the first parliamentary by-election contest, when the Social

Democrats' popularity and voter appeal could be checked against those of the Labour and Tory parties. The Warrington by-election was in many ways decisive for the future.

Chapter Eighteen

WARRINGTON

When the Member of Parliament for Warrington, Sir Tom Williams, accepted the appointment of circuit judge, it was the signal for a by-election, the first for over a year, and the first since the formation of the Social Democratic Party two months before.

This ought to have been a cause for Social Democrat rejoicing, a chance to prove themselves at the polls in an election where real votes are counted, leaving behind the opinion polls which, while interesting, are only an indication of possible reality.

But the Social Democrats, though keen to get going and to keep up the momentum of their early campaign, were unsure. Warrington was not an ideal seat to fight, being a Labour stronghold in the North West. To win would be almost impossible. Even to put up a good showing very unlikely.

According to the Social Democrats' own calculations, Warrington was about number 550 in their scale of winnable constituencies. The previous result had given Labour a massive 61.6% share of the vote, while the Liberal showing, at 9%, was weaker than their national average. So what to do about Warrington? To ignore it would be to lay the SDP open to the charge of lacking political conviction. The Social Democrats had to be seen fighting and putting their ideas across to the electorate.

Possible failure posed a great risk for the Social Democrats so early on in their development. To involve one of the new Party leaders as candidate was to put his or her personal reputation on the line. The Party hesitated and was seen to do so, potentially even more damaging than failure. At first there was talk of fielding a second-rank candidate. David Williams, the son of Sir Tom Williams, himself a convert to the Social Democratic cause and a man with local connnections, declared himself ready to stand. David Marquand, former Labour MP and highly thought of by those around him, was

166

another possibility.

However, there was pressure for one of the stars to stand. The Liberals made it clear that their support would only be forthcoming if Shirley Williams or Roy Jenkins were to stand. Shirley Williams, after a period of considerable thought, decided not to stand, in spite of the fact that at least one opinion poll, carried out by the Sun newspaper, suggested that she could win the seat with a sizeable majority.

The spotlight then shifted to Roy Jenkins. It was not essential for the prestige of the Party or for the future of the SDP/Liberal alliance that Jenkins should stand, but pressures were exerted by the party, by the Liberal allies, and not least by the media. Jenkins, whatever his private reservations, accepted the challenge. Perhaps, he did so as much for his own personal good as for that of his party. Even his friends were saying that he needed to get his feet wet. Having been out of British politics for years, he needed to prove his mettle. Better to fight in Warrington and lose than not to fight at all. If he were to pull off the miracle and win, the bonus would be an almost automatic claim to the leadership of the party. In fact, he came out of the contest strengthened. The man who had been criticised for being easy-going turned out to be a tough politician, prepared to fight. The expatriate was again at the centre of the British political scene.

The start of the campaign for what was being billed as the by-election of the century brought people from all the parties to Warrington. Tories who wanted only to avoid the humiliation of a lost deposit (which they failed to do), and Labour people on their mission of mortally wounding the newly-created monster, to use the words of Peter Shore. All were fired with the feeling, expressed by Shakespeare's Henry V at Agincourt that: "Gentlemen in England now abed, shall think themselves accurs'd they were not here." It goes without saying that all the Social Democrat leaders were in town to support Roy Jenkins. Most of the SDP MPs came up, as well as Lord George-Brown and Dick Taverne. From the Liberal party, David Steel gave support; so did Cyril Smith. The Tories had to steer a middle way, show support for their candidate but not sink too much prestige in a lost cause; the Home Secretary, Willie Whitelaw, and the Defence Secretary, John Nott, were there.

In the Labour camp, MPs of all shades joined in: Eric Heffer, Neil Kinnock, Peter Shore, Gerald Kaufman. So did Harold Wilson. So did Michael Foot. If Michael Foot drew the largest single audience of 700 people, the Social Democrat stars, Owen, Williams, Rodgers, not to mention Jenkins, consistently drew the best meetings - of up to 500 at a time, which for politicial meetings in today's TV age is most unusual.

The candidates themselves were an interesting, though not wholly appropriate set of party representatives. Of Roy Jenkins himself it was continually said that he was the wrong choice for a northern industrial town, that his manner was remote, academic, too middle-class, out of tune with the workers. The fact that he had been a successful MP for twenty years or so for a Birmingham constituency was often ignored. Stan Sorrell, the Conservative candidate, was the Vice-Chairman of Margaret Thatcher's own constituency party. But rather more quoted was the fact that he was a London bus driver, though, as someone was quick to notice, he drove a number 13!

The Labour candidate who made it into the House was Douglas Hoyle. His credentials were left-wing: MP till 1979 in neighbouring Nelson and Colne, President of his Union, ASTMS until just before his nomination and subsequently vice-president, and a member of Labour's NEC. Precisely the sort of candidate most suitable for the Social Democrats to fight, personifying the left-wing tendency and making clear the new party's *raison d'etre*.

There was also a large field of eccentric also-rans, including the ubiquitous 77-year-old, Lieutenant-Commander William Boaks (Public Safety, Democratic Monarchist, White Residents), now in his twenty-first election campaign, who picked up his normal modest crop of votes, this time fourteen. D A Keane was fighting as one of the other Social Democrats, who had previously challenged the national Social Democrats in the lawcourts, claiming the party name, but had lost. As a result, one of their number changed his name to Roy Harold Jenkins, proposing to run as the third Social Democrat and second Roy Jenkins, only to have his by-election nomination rejected by Warrington's acting Returning Officer. (Shortly after the Warrington by-election, the second Roy Jenkins was planning to change his name yet again, so that he could fight Shirley Williams as Shirley Williams No. 2 in the by-election where No. 1 would be standing).

But the fight in Warrington was always going to be between Jenkins and Hoyle, between the SDP and Labour. As observers of the scene noted, Warrington was not so much a constituency where people had strong political convictions, though doubtless many did, but rather a close knit community where "Labour is built into the framework, like the terraced houses, the Catholic clubs, the wireworks, soapworks and breweries ... The SDP is the stranger in the interlocking society" (*Guardian*, 13 July 1981). The SDP's problem was to break into this community loyalty.

No middle-class constituency this. Six out of seven of the electorate were blue collar workers, half of them unskilled. As elsewhere in the country and particularly in the urban North, Warrington found itself with over 14% unemployed. People were desperately worried. Inevitably, unemployment was the political issue on which candidates concentrated.

The Labour case was that Common Market membership was the cause: since Britain joined the EEC, unemployment had risen by a staggering 432%. Labour was the only party proposing to withdraw from Europe. Moreover, Jenkins, as the newly returned President of the Commission in Brussels, could be personally tarred with that brush.

Jenkins, on the other hand, pointed to increasing unemployment under both previous governments: a 50% increase under Labour 1974-79, and under the Tories 1979-81 an additional 160%. Where the Social Democrats were often criticised for not offering specific policies, Jenkins offered a detailed package to counter unemployment. Not intended as a cure-all, it was a scheme to create up to a million jobs. In the absence of magic wands during a deep recession, the scheme was generally well received, though the *Guardian* pointed out that Jenkins, "Perhaps too engrossed in the complexities of his argument, tended to make involved discourses of his platform speeches and the night he announced his plan to take a million off the dole he almost lost the audience before he got to the essentials."

The Tory candidate, Stan Sorrell, who concentrated on law and order, was never a serious rival. It was always assumed he would finish third, a victim of national Tory policies.

The main contest had to be between party defender and party challenger, between Labour and SDP. So while the country was exuberantly putting up pictures of Prince Charles and Lady Diana and getting ready for the Royal Wedding later that month, and while others were rioting in the streets of Liverpool and Manchester, throwing stones and petrol bombs, Warrington concentrated on its own destiny. Excitement was limited to political speeches, heckling and canvassing, the Social Democrat Punch and Judy show.

Although the SDP were not ready to give chapter and verse on the details of their policies, their overall views became quite clear. At home, to fight unemployment, and retain a mixed economy; abroad to remain in the EEC, to seek multilateral disarmament and to give real support to the Third World, in line with the Brandt Commission recommendations; to promote consensus as opposed to confrontation politics and to introduce electoral reform through a system of proportional representation.

The Social Democrats fought Labour above all on its extremist attitudes and left-wing policies of unilateral disarmament, withdrawal from the Common Market, siege economy and further nationalisation. Doug Hoyle's curriculum vitae helped them identify Labour policies with him personally: Hoyle was to refer to this as an exceptional smear campaign. For his part, Hoyle campaigned in low key, not dwelling on the Left/Right problems within Labour, and refusing to be drawn on the subject of Benn, Healey or Silkin as candidates for the Deputy Leadership of the Party. Immediately after his victory, Hoyle reported to the Shadow Cabinet that the Benn candidature had proved a major and recurring problem in his campaign.

At the time, when suggestions were made that he was an extremist, Hoyle responded that he was a moderate man, cuddly and affectionate. While many took him at face value, others saw him differently. *The Times* described him as "curmudgeonly"; a hurried look in the Oxford Dictionary, indicated that this meant 'churlish, miserly fellow'.

As the votes were counted on the evening of 16 July and the result announced in the early minutes of 17 July, the country waited expectantly. Would "the Social Democrat monster have been strangled at birth", or would "the face of British politics never be the same again" as Jenkins believed possible.

The result made history. A safe Labour seat had become a marginal. The new party - whose members in Warrington at the start of the campaign had numbered thirteen - had moved up from nowhere into a close second place. Jenkins, the loser by only 1,759 votes, was jubilant - the real victor of Warrington. No one had predicted this result. Opinion polls had consistently given the Social Democrats a more modest support. Labour had predicted a clear-cut victory for its candidate. Even the Social Democrats were astounded by their own success. The election commentator, the late Robert Mackenzie, with the help of the BBC computer, made projections which showed that if the Warrington swing were repeated on a national scale, the Social Democrat/Liberal Alliance would win an unbelievable 503 seats in the House of Commons, leaving 113 seats to Labour and the even more amazing figure of just one seat for the Conservatives. As Rodgers subsequently commented, apart from being unlikely, such a result would be bad for democracy.

The results as announced and compared with the General Election were:

Douglas Hoyle (Labour) 14,280; **Roy Jenkins** (Social Democrat with Liberal Party Support) 12,521; **Stanley Sorrell** (Conservative) 2,102; **W G Boaks** (Public Safety, Democratic Monarchist, White Residents) 14; **N S Chantreel** (Ecology Party) 219; **R H Fleming** (Independent Labour Party) 53; **D Hussey** (United Democratic Labour Party) 38; **T L Keen** (Campaign for Prosperous Britain) 10; **I Leslie** (Citizens' Band Radio Party) 111; **H Wise** (English Democratic Party) 11
Turnout: 67.02%
Percentages of Poll:

Labour	48.3
Social Democrat	42.4
Conservative	7

Labour Majority 1,759

The Conservative candidate lost his deposit.

General Election
Sir Tom Williams (Labour-Coop) 19,306; **G Povey** (Conservative) 9,032; **I B Browne** (Liberal) 2,833; **C Campbell** (Social Democrat) 155
Labour Majority 10,274

The main parties' shares of the votes, compared with the 1979 General Election were as follows:

	1981	1979	Difference
	%	%	%
SDP/Liberal	42.4	9.0(Lib)	+33.4
Labour	48.4	61.6	-13.2
Tory	7.1	28.8	-21.7

171

A staggering result but of course dramatic by-election swings against the major parties had happened before. Certainly in 1972/3, halfway through the previous Conservative administration, Liberal candidates had made startling progress, also slashing both Conservative and Labour votes. In July 1973, in the Isle of Ely, where no Liberal had stood at the previous election, Liberal Clement Freud won with 38.3% of the vote. Likewise in Sutton and Cheam, in December 1972, a Liberal took the seat from the Conservatives, with a 38.9% increase. But, perhaps a comparison with the northern constituency by-elections of Chester-le-Street, March 1973, and Manchester Exchange, June 1973, is more revealing. Both were Labour strongholds. Under normal circumstances Labour should have cashed in on the Conservative Government's unpopularity. No Liberal had stood at the previous election in either constituency. Labour held the seats but the Liberal won respectively 38.6% and 36.5% of the poll, taking votes from both main parties. Though more of these came from the Tories, they could console themselves that swings against the party of goverment are normal. Labour had no such consolation.

Although Labour's humiliation while in opposition had precedents, Warrington was different. Labour's worst result for half a century was due to a Party not four months old. Whatever else might be said, 'the monster' was alive and well. Nevertheless, Labour could justifiably point to Chester-le-Street and show that three elections later that seat remained Labour.

So, while one Warrington did not guarantee national success, neither could it be dismissed as insignificant. The SDP had won 42.4% of the vote, following earlier polls in Warrington which showed SDP support running at between 27% and 33%, and rising gradually toward the end of the campaign. The Social Democrats would have considered anything over 30% good and Shirley Williams noted her own personal forecast in her diary at 36% and thought herself too optimistic; the result far exceeded the Party's genuine expectations. Minutes after the result was announced, Jenkins summed up: "I have taken part in twelve elections. This is the first I have lost in thirty-five years, but it is by far the greatest victory in which I have ever participated."

After Warrington, the SDP could no longer be dismissed simply as a media creation. Neither could the argument be maintained that new parties have no future. Overnight it had

become possible to think in terms of a Social
Democratic/Liberal government. The very fact of being a
realistic proposition enhanced the possibility itself. One of the
main barriers which had always confronted the Liberal Party
was voters' conviction that a Liberal vote was a wasted vote.
From now on people could vote Social Democrat as they would
for one of the major parties. After Warrington, it was evident
that a vote for the Alliance was meaningful.

Another by-product of Warrington was a stronger
Alliance. Before, it had consisted largely of the leaders of the
two parties getting together. Now, Liberal and SDP workers
had descended on Warrington, all keen to prove that the new
left-of-centre Alliance could change the face of British politics.
Mostly young, all enthusiastic, they found they actually got on
well together. Warrington was important to them personally
as well as to their parties. The election result was the reward
which made their joint work more meaningful.

Furthermore, the Social Democrats appreciated the
devoted support of the Liberals. It was one thing for the new
party to get behind its own candidate; it was clearly more
selfless for the Liberals to put in similar energy.

The price of the Liberals' support was the principle of
'Buggins' turn'. The parties agreed in theory to fight alternate
by-elections, except in special circumstances. Rather than
fight each other, the parties would put their joint weight
behind each other's campaign. However, this agreement of
principle was to lead to complications in the next by-election in
Croydon North-West, as could easily have been predicted. As
an arrangement 'Buggins' turn' was only intended to serve
short-term needs until a more sophisticated system could be
worked out.

Chapter Nineteen

THE LIBERAL CONNECTION

When the Liberals met in Llandudno in September 1981, they voted overwhelmingly in favour of an SDP/Liberal alliance: 1,600 for and 112 against. The working relationship which existed between the two parties had now been given the democratic blessing of grassroots Liberals. Although expected, this verdict could not have been taken for granted, given the independence of spirit or even cussedness for which the Liberal membership was noted. By its huge majority of fourteen to one, the vote underpinned David Steel's leadership and the alliance crucial to both the SDP and the Liberal Party as the recipe for political power. As a result David Steel could, without blushing or being accused of letting his imagination run away with him, end his keynote speech with the words: "I have the good fortune to be the first Liberal leader for over half an century who is able to say to you at the end of our annual assembly: go back to your constituencies and prepare for government."

Without the alliance neither SDP nor Liberals, fighting independently, and fighting one another, could have hoped for power, as all those present at the conference must have known. Yet there were those who felt deeply that an alliance represented a threat to the character and principles of their party. A minority found it difficult to swallow the idea of throwing in their lot with the 'Soggy Dems', politicians whom they had been fighting when these were carrying out Labour policies. Geoffrey Roberts, Liberal councillor in London's Shoreditch, spoke of Social Democrats as unsuitable colleagues for lifelong Liberals, referring to them as "Yesterday's men, from the sixties and seventies", and to the alliance as a "trick to get elected without doing any work." Councillor Derek Morse was less happy about some of the SDP recruits than he was about the Gang of Four: "The veneer may look good but the woodwork may be rotten." But the leadership as well as the majority of those attending, while

174

making warning noises about the need to proceed with care, took the view of Clement Freud: "It's like seeing the light and calling in the electrician to check the voltage."

From the earliest discussions between Jenkins and Steel, around the time of the Dimbleby lecture two years earlier, it was clear that Jenkins, sometimes perceived as a Liberal manque, and Steel, often seen as a radical social democrat, had much in common. They were in broad agreement about the main issues of the day and got on well together. Jenkins was said to have been dissuaded by Steel from joining the Liberal Party on the grounds that a two-party centre grouping would have more impact on national politics and that the launching of a new party was a likelier route to power.

In the days following the Dimbleby lecture, Liberals and future Social Democrats sniffed at one another and found they had more in common than not. There was little of substance which separated them on policy. They found they got on in human terms. The atmosphere in which they talked was in marked contrast to the uncomradely spirit the Social Democrats had become used to inside the Labour Party.

An early and secret conference held in the West Country, which confirmed to both sides that there was more uniting them than separating them, took place during the weekend of 26/27 January 1980 at the homes of Chairman of the Liberal Party, Roger Pincham and Clive Lindley, three times his Labour opponent in Leominster, Herefordshire. Ten Liberals, including Viv Bingham, the President-elect, and Cyril Carr, leader of the Liverpool Liberals, conferred with a similar number of social democrats, including former Labour MP Michael Barnes, Jim Daly, and Professor Don Swift, Vice Chancellor of the Open University. The re-alignment of British politics under discussion was to happen sooner and more dramatically than could have been expected by even the most optimistic participants.

In September in Blackpool, at the annual Liberal Assembly, David Marquand, seen there as a Roy Jenkins' emissary, addressed a fringe meeting packed to overflowing. An understanding between Liberals and social democrats, he said, was crucial to the future of the British Left, and concluded that David Steel, Roy Jenkins, Shirley Williams, Bill Rodgers and David Owen were the natural leaders of such a coalition. Although the Assembly chairman, Michael Meadowcroft and others were guarded in their response, this was a significant milestone on the way to the Alliance.

In January the Limehouse Declaration was made. From the start, opinion polls showed that an alliance was essential if the new political initiative was to succeed. Together, SDP and Liberals overcame the hidden obstacle of the wasted vote, separately they would still only function as mini-parties with no chance of rivalling Labour or Tory Parties.

By 16 June 1981 the two parties made their joint public statement: 'A Fresh Start for Britain'. Although, as the *Guardian* pointed out, it was in the main "a broad declaration apparently in favour of virtue and opposed to sin", it was a formal declaration of intent for a working alliance on the road to government. Shirley Williams and David Steel were joint chairmen of the working party responsible for the document, which included Richard Holmes and Roger Pincham for the Liberals and William Rodgers and David Marquand for the Social Democrats. For months, David Steel had been urging Social Democrats to agree to a working partnership, sometimes to the point of irritating David Owen; but for Steel both partnership and timing were important if he was to obtain his party's approval for an alliance. That had to be at the September annual assembly in Llandudno.

The final paragraph of 'Fresh Start for Britain' was the crux of the matter. It states that "our two parties wish to avoid fighting each other in elections" and refers to "electoral arrangements in our respective parties which will make an alliance effective". It was, of course, nitty-gritty details of electoral arrangements which brought some problems. The Alliance required some kind of parity which members in both parties found troublesome. Was parity justified? The Social Democrats brought with them former cabinet and junior ministers, who between them displayed an impressive experience of government. They also knew that the Liberals on their own were an interesting party but literally powerless. The magic ingredient, the dynamic new dimension was, without question, the addition of the new party.

For their part, the Liberals, having soldiered on for thirty-six post-war years, saw the equation from their own point of view. They had nearly been extinguished as a political party. Yet, over the years, they had clawed their way back to respectability and public recognition. Though they could claim no recent experience of government, apart from the brief and delicate influence they had exercised in the Lib-Lab pact with Callaghan, they had the pride of a party which by 1974 had won the support of six million people. They had also developed their own style of community politics in recent years, with special emphasis being given to local issues.

They had a national organisation on the ground in the constituencies, which the Social Democrats initially lacked. Shirley Williams was not without sympathy when she referred to "the parable of the belated labourers in the vineyard, paid as much for joining in the last hour as for working throughout the dust and heat of the day."

It was clearly going to be crucial to the Alliance that the new SDP should not ride roughshod over Liberal sensitivities. There should be no question of an unequal marriage, for, in the words of one with vested interests, chairman of the Conservative Party, Cecil Parkinson, this was a marriage between "a Liberal mouse and an SDP boa-constrictor" and there was "no known case of a mouse eating a boa-constrictor."

Nevertheless, it was the Social Democrats who were worried that they would lose out in the forthcoming division of constituencies. The Liberals, already entrenched in the plum constituencies, were apparently trying to steal a march on their new partners by speeding up the process of selecting their own candidates, before the SDP could organise its first local parties, let alone field SDP candidates. Steel's own attempt to restrain local Liberals was resented by some, since this was bound to run counter to the central Liberal tradition of power in the regions, of independence, decentralisation and democracy. Steel's threat to disown rebel candidates provoked the wrath of die-hard Liberals, not least of all the larger-than-life MP for Rochdale, Cyril Smith, who said: "I don't believe that the Liberal Party is the sort of party in which constituencies will be dictated to by the central bureaucracy in London. Any attempt to enforce that will be catastrophic."

Still, by mid-September, the Liberals had already selected 250 candidates. They were also understandably proprietorial about the seventy-eight constituencies where, in the 1979 general election, Liberals had come second. Only in two of these were Liberals second to Labour; in all the rest they came second to the Conservatives. So the SDP could see itself fighting the tough seats, where Labour MPs had massive majorities, while the Liberal allies were going to contest the soft under-belly of Conservatism requiring, on the whole, smaller swings for victory.

The system of Buggins' turn for fighting by-elections

just about worked initially - each party taking turns to contest vacant seats. Jenkins fought Warrington. Pitt fought North West Croydon for the Liberals and Shirley Williams won Crosby for the Social Democrats. But even then the sensitivities of the Liberals in both Croydon and Crosby were ruffled, particularly in Croydon. However, once agreement had been reached, the allies gave magnificent support to the contesting party. In practice, the Alliance functioned well on the ground and what gave added stimulus was the pay-off in the polling booths. The Alliance was winning. It was particularly important that both parties should be making progress in parallel and that neither should feel like the country cousin. When Bill Pitt stood his ground and fought Croydon North West, not only was this a triumph for the Alliance, to turn a lost deposit in 1979 to a victory in 1981, but it was essential for Liberal self-respect within the Alliance: a run-of-the-mill Liberal could hold his own with SDP glamour stars like Jenkins and Williams. For the SDP to have a chance of winning power, paradoxically, the Alliance had to come first, which is why the Liberal victory in Croydon was important.

After Crosby, the Alliance approach to elections changed. A joint working party divided the country into thirty-two separate bargaining units. Each consisted of between sixteen and twenty constituencies. London accounted for four units. The objective was to achieve overall parity, with Liberals and Social Democrats each fielding around three hundred parliamentary candidates; parity was likewise the objective within each bargaining unit. But it was agreed that within each unit a ratio of three to two would be acceptable, to take account of special factors - the known strength of Liberals in the West Country, for example.

The first unit negotiations took place in December 1981, with a view to reaching final agreement by 31 March 1982. Indeed, the first local agreements were reached in record time. Nottinghamshire was shared out to the satisfaction of both parties within a mere two-hour session, and Derbyshire shared out the same weekend.

Although sitting MPs, whether SDP or Liberal, were to have priority, some refugees from the Labour Party expecting to take their place automatically as SDP MPs might not be acceptable. A number were seen as unwelcome opportunists, and Bill Rodgers had also given notice that after 31 December 1981, defectors would have to take their chance against other candidates. Some tough negotiations must still lie ahead. In the words of pro-Alliance Liberal candidate, Claire Brooks: "You don't go to the bargaining table and lie down and say, 'Here I am, take me'."

At the turn of the year, the first major row threatened good relations. Bill Rodgers, heading up the SDP negotiating team, unilaterally suspended talks on electoral divisions, claiming that the Liberals had not been negotiating within the spirit or the letter of the agreement. The Derbyshire share-out which had gone so smoothly had subsequently run into trouble at local Liberal level.

Also, the Liberals in Greenock and Port Glasgow were refusing to adopt the sitting MP, Dr J Dickson Mabon, a recent Labour defector, saying "We fought against him for twenty-five years and the scars of those contests are still there." Instead, they were insisting on their own candidate, Alan Blair, the leader of the Inverclyde District Council. They were supported by the Liberal leadership in Scotland, who claimed that national guidelines did not apply to Scotland and that all Scottish SDP MPs could be challenged.

The row which Rodgers had deliberately created had an immediate effect. Rodgers and Steel hammered out a more precise agreement. Liberals would be allowed the top fifty preference constituencies, while the SDP could select one hundred of the next one hundred and fifty. This new parity between the parties, giving each a prior claim on one hundred of two hundred constituencies would, it was hoped, be accepted by the local Liberals. At the same time, David Steel isolated the Greenock problem as one which would have to be resolved quite separately in the future and should not be allowed to impede the overall negotiations which were quickly resumed. However, Liberals and SDP had been seen in serious conflict publicly for the first time.

In the meantime, the two parties had been co-operating admirably for the council elections. Perhaps because more vacancies were available, disputes did not mar the atmosphere. A share-out of power could take place fairly and easily.

For Liberals to be thinking about power was itself the great transformation. No longer need the Liberal Party be the party of principles but no influence, of protest but no power. The decades in the wilderness were ending. Only five years before in Llandudno, in his first speech as leader, David Steel had stated that he did not intend to lead "just a nice debating society". He had then upset many present by announcing that he was prepared to consider sharing power with other parties. There were, of course, historical precedents. The Liberal Party had often sought alliances to improve in political fortunes.

Former Liberal leader Jo Grimond had made his pitch for a coalition of the progressive left. In 1965 when Harold Wilson's Labour Government was struggling on a majority of three and later of one, Grimond had used a party political broadcast to suggest a coalition with a radical programme. Wilson, judging correctly that Labour's fortunes would improve, was not tempted, as Gaitskell had not been tempted earlier. In 1959, when analysing reasons for Labour's third successive defeat, Gaitskell had dismissed the idea of a pact with the Liberals: "We can toss that one out of the window. There is no evidence that it would do us any good." So twenty years went by before an electoral partnership was deemed to do good.

A precedent did exist though, for an electoral pact between the parties, between the then mighty Liberals and the newly-born Labour Party, still known under its original name of Labour Representation Committee (LRC). That electoral pact of 1903, whereby Labour and Liberals avoided fighting each other in certain constituencies, directly resulted in each party winning more seats at the subsequent election of 1906. At its birth in 1900, the LRC had already agreed "to co-operate with any party which for the time being may be engaged in promoting legislation in the direct interest of labour." Keir Hardie, present at that inaugural conference, said, to echoes of "hear, hear", that if there was any prospect of a working agreement with the official Liberal Party, nothing in his past career would lead him to hinder it. So a pact was made, albeit a secret one, three years later in 1903.

The negotiators were the Liberal Chief Whip, Herbert Gladstone, son of the great Liberal leader, and Ramsay MacDonald, the first secretary of the LRC, himself elected MP for the first time in 1906. Secrecy was deemed necessary lest the pact offend either wing of the LRC, the socialist militants or conservative working men.

It was just the sort of arrangement which would emerge eighty-one years later, on the principle of 'You don't stand here, we won't stand there'. And it worked magnificently, enabling both parties to swell their numbers in the House of Commons. In the subsequent General Election of 1906, the Liberals won a landslide victory and went on to form a memorable government, one of the two greatest reforming administrations of the century, the other being the Attlee government of 1945. Labour's gains were decisive for the Party's early development: In 1900 the LRC, just seven months old, had only won two seats. Now it won twenty-nine seats. But twenty-four of these had been unopposed by the Liberals. The electoral pact had been crucial. The 1981 nationwide electoral pact would be no less vital for success.

Furthermore, the Alliance could see a specific example of what happens in the event of a breakdown in the pact. Just as in 1981 Scottish Liberals were claiming the right to break free from the national pact, so in 1906 the pact worked least well in Scotland. As *The Times* reported on 15 January 1906, commenting on the election results: "Scotland, however, is not nearly so strong in Labour representatives as England and Wales. It has returned only two, and the fact is significant, being largely due to a number of triangular contests in which Liberals and Labour split the anti-Unionist vote. It is evidence of division between them, and has caused considerable irritation." The problem then as now was how to restrain the constituencies from action independent of the party centres. Gladstone had stated: "... I have no doubt that I could come to terms with the leaders of the Labour party in the course of half a morning ... The difficulty lies with the constituencies themselves." An understanding had become increasingly important as Labour candidates had been splitting the progressive vote, enabling Conservatives to win.

The consideration uppermost in Herbert Gladstone's mind was whether for the Liberals the price of success at the polls would be too high. Ought the Liberal party to prefer defeat rather than assist in any way in fostering the growing power of the Labour Party? Gladstone had no doubts that there would be an appreciable gain in Liberal and LRC seats, to the detriment of the Conservatives. Indeed, in 1906, following the Liberal and LRC election successes, Gladstone's secretary Jesse Herbert wrote: "Was there ever such a justification of a policy by results?" But was the cost too great? Was the subsequent rise of the Labour Party brought about by the Liberals' own short-sighted action? Or was the Labour Party pre-destined to grow with the rise of the working classes? Did the Liberal-Labour pact hasten the near demise of the Liberal party? Before the first world war, Labour's rise did not seem quite so sure. It had many reverses, largely because the Liberal Government was stealing its thunder with reforming legislation, and its own role was difficult to

181

establish. Certainly Liberalism enjoyed its greatest triumphs after the electoral pact, before the inexorable post-first-world-war decline set in. In fact, the pact probably had little influence on the later fortunes of the Liberals or Labour. Yet Liberals today might be excused for posing the same questions.

However, the 1981 Alliance is national and its benefits should be proportionately greater than in 1906. Today's Liberal party, a shadow of its earlier self, can only gain from such an arrangement. The planned introduction of proportional representation will be the big prize for both parties.

Questions for the 1980s occupying some minds in the Social Democratic and Liberal parties include: Will one party emerge the stronger? Will it be able to influence the character of the other? Decisions about mergers between the two need not and have not yet been taken, but this must be a possibility. Clearly an alliance which has won the support of millions will need to keep faith with the electorate. In one form or another, the Alliance must continue. The main difference between the past electoral pact and the present one is not only that the first was secret, but that the second implicitly involves the electorate.

To quote David Steel at Llandudno again: "Political parties normally seek to persuade the public to follow them. For the last months the voice of the public, as registered in the polls, has been desperately pleading with our two political parties. Their message has been: 'Get together for our sake.' The 1981 electoral pact is not only an internal pact between parties, it is a pact with the people."

Chapter Twenty

FROM WARRINGTON ONWARDS

Continued Alliance gains during 1981 proved beyond doubt that it was a serious contender for power. Roy Jenkins' 'my greatest victory' speech after Warrington could not be discounted as hyperbole.

Predictions made by politicians like Jo Grimond, Roy Jenkins and Dick Taverne for a decade or more - that the British people were waiting to vote for a centre radical party seriously in the running for government - were proved correct. The support had always been there. It now emerged, undoubtedly strengthened by the extreme behaviour of the Labour and Conservative parties.

On 26 November Shirley Williams returned to the House of Commons as the first elected Social Democrat. Her victory in a by-election at Crosby, previously a rock-safe Tory seat, turned a 19,000 Conservative majority into a 5,000 majority for the SDP. In 1979 a Liberal had polled 15.2% of the vote. Shirley Williams now polled 49%.

The previous month, on 22 October, the bread-and-butter candidate, Liberal Bill Pitt had won Croydon North West, the first Liberal Alliance candidate to win a seat. He had stood three times before and this time converted a lost deposit into a convincing win. The Liberal vote had been quadrupled to 40%.

Crosby, Croydon and Warrington, though quite different constituencies - safe Tory, mixed Labour and Tory, and traditional Labour - had reacted to the new Alliance impetus in remarkably similar ways. The consistency of the pattern underlined the new political reality.

	Warrington 16 July 81	Croydon NW 22 Oct 81	Crosby 26 Nov 81
Alliance vote	42.4%	40%	49%
increase over Lib vote in 79	33.4%	29.5%	33.9%

The Alliance's electoral support during the second half of 1981 settled at 40 to 50% - a figure corroborated by both opinion polls and local council elections.

At council by-elections, half the seats were initially falling to the Alliance. By the end of the year no less than two thirds were going to the Alliance. From Croydon onwards the Alliance was polling 46% of the vote.

Islington was the first borough to go Social Democrat. All three local MP's left the Labour Party, two to join the SDP and one as Independent Labour. Labour councillors defected *en masse*. Although many of the new Islington SDP representatives were criticised for being less than pure idealists and more like Labour apparatchiks, the first town hall was now flying the flag of Social Democracy.

By the end of the year, there was a solid block of thirty-nine Alliance MPs in the House of Commons. Of these, twenty-seven were Social Democrats, of whom seven represented London constituencies.

The two old parties were in the meantime showing signs of strain; the new political situation with its dangers of electoral disaster was making Conservative and Labour politicians react.

While Mrs Thatcher still kept to her tune of TINA - There Is No Alternative, to the Conservative economic strategy, party voices were heard suggesting that there were alternatives. Reflation to stimulate the economy and help people back to work was being recommended by Edward Heath, Geoffrey Rippon, Norman St John Stevas and Sir Ian Gilmour from among known opponents inside the Party. Rippon's name was even being canvassed as possible replacement leader. More surprisingly, a number of loyal members of Mrs Thatcher's Cabinet, in carefully coded speeches at the annual conference, were saying precisely the same thing. Francis Pym and Michael Heseltine were also advocating reflation to avert electoral disaster.

Eight Young Conservatives joined the SDP. Rippon did not contest the leadership. Mrs Thatcher remained firmly in control. The Government did make money available to help the young unemployed but the basic monetarist policy remained. Economically, 1982 was beginning to look slightly more hopeful, though unemployment and inflation prospects remained bleak.

In the meantime, Labour's continuous movement to the left was interrupted. Both at the annual TUC conference and

184

at the Party conference in Brighton, the Right organised itself
and made important advances. In so far as this was true, it
also caused a hiccup in the continued advance of the Social
Democratic Party. Had there been a further violent lurch to
the left at Brighton, the SDP might have received a larger
contingent of Labour MP refugees than the few who switched
over in the aftermath of the conference.

Although the Party consolidated around left-wing
policies, the Right had a number of important successes. The
NEC changed complexion, moving right, against the trend of
the past decade. The 'broad church', 'unity first' contingent
won out, a mixture of soft left Tribunites and right-wingers
won marginal control. Eric Varley, after years of attempting to
win the post of Treasurer for the Right, now did so, ousting
Norman Atkinson.

Denis Healey remained Deputy Leader. Benn, the chief
challenger came within less than one percent of winning.
Controversy characterised the election.

The TGWU (accounting for 8% of the total vote), having
consulted its membership which wanted Healey, proceeded to
vote for Silkin on the first ballot and Benn on the second. Two
days before the election the *New Statesman* leader stated:
"The issue for the TGWU delegation is no longer about the
merits of the candidates. If a consultation for this or any other
contest had shown support for King Kong, Genghis Khan or
Margaret Thatcher, the point would be the same: democracy is
worthless unless you are willing to accept unpalatable
results."

Benn would have won, had the soft Left not abstained.
Nearly thirty left-wing MPs did not vote for Benn, though
there was no disagreement on policy. Bennites, having been
robbed of victory by their own former allies, were bitter. In
December, after nine Labour MPs who had voted for Healey
had crossed over to the SDP, Benn declared himself Deputy
Leader of the Labour Party. Would Benn exercise his
democratic right and put the Party through another deputy
leadership contest in 1982, to make his statement reality?

The truth of the matter was that both the Labour Party
annual conference and the Benn/Healey/Silkin vote showed
two parties within the party, still bitterly in conflict. The
Bennites even considered regrouping under the new/old
standard of 'Labour Representation Committee'. For all that,
even some of the hard Left were beginning to soft-pedal on
their demands to purify the Party on their terms, conscious of

185

the forthcoming general elections.

Nevertheless Labour finished 1981 with its most controversial moves. Eight years after the end of proscription, during which time the undemocratic Left had operated unmolested inside the Party and entryism had become a much-used word, and when Marxists outside were returning to a Labour Party they could feel in tune with, the Party acted, divided as usual, but finally acted.

The immediate cause for action was 29-year-old Peter Tatchell. Following Robert Mellish's decision not to stand in Bermondsey again, the local Labour Party had selected as candidate Tatchell who, though not a Militant, was of the far Left and typical of the new breed of dedicated Labour workers intent on irreversably changing Britain. Michael Foot, after sustained pressure from the right wing of his party, chose this case for an emotional confrontation with the extreme Left, staking his reputation and his role as leader.

Yet Tatchell was not the most obvious choice as a sticking point for Labour and for Foot. Militants had been selected elsewhere and approved by the NEC. Trotskyist infiltration had been allowed to continue undisturbed, in spite of Reg Underhill's warning reports in 1975 and 1980. Now Tatchell had advocated extra-parliamentary action; some had argued that this meant anti-parliamentary, while Tatchell himself claimed that it meant what it said - action to supplement, not replace, parliamentary democracy.

To many observers, Tatchell seemed not unlike Michael Foot himself. As Peter Jenkins put it in the *Guardian* (9 December 1981): "... television viewers might be excused for supposing that Mr Foot himself, although a Parliament man *par excellence*, in fact spends most of his time on the streets." Extra-parliamentary protest and action were a time-honoured Labour tradition. The Tatchell affair had to be seen as a choice between party purification to improve electoral prospects, and considerations of Tatchell and the Bermondsey Labour Party. The NEC duly rejected Tatchell as Bermondsey candidate. Tatchell had not been allowed to state his case.

At this time, Foot won two additional battles. With his personal prestige at stake, the NEC agreed by a narrow margin to investigate the Militant Tendency. The application of Trotskyist, Tariq Ali to join the Party was rejected. Foot's actions, intended to bind the party together and give it electoral appeal, clearly ran counter to his own instincts and to those of many in the Party. The splits became wider, accompanied by the Left's cries of 'witch-hunt'.

From the unusually long list of seven, Jim Mortimer was chosen as the new General Secretary of the Labour Party. The appointment of Mortimer, previously the head of ACAS, the conciliation body, seemed a symbolic act.

The SDP, however, had no need of conciliation. Followers appeared to be in accord with leadership on policy. The SDP's rolling annual conference, taking members from Perth to Bradford to London by special SDP train, left them triumphant that in their world of rational people, all problems could be resolved by discussion.

SDP policy was debated at the three conferences. Papers were read on main policies, on foreign affairs, economic policy, housing, industrial and trade union relations, education, and on the party constitution. Roy Jenkins made proposals to reflate the economy, with an inflationary tax to penalise those creating the inflation - proposals which were met with general approval. But nothing could be decided till a constitution was agreed and approved by the party membership in 1982. One of the main controversies of the whole conference and of the constitutional question was the leadership - would this be decided by the parliamentary party or the membership as a whole?

Although observers noted that most of the participants were middle-class, the party could console itself with the 40 to 50% voting support it was attaining. SDP voters were a genuine cross-section of the population.

Later, in the autumn of 1981, a poll carried out by Opinion Research Ltd for London Weekend Television's *Weekend World* confirmed that the membership was broadly in step with the leadership on important home and foreign policies. Based on over 5,500 completed questionnaires, the research showed that the party was indeed a party of moderate reform.

There was overwhelming agreement about staying in Europe, controlled reflation, an incomes policy, the mixed economy, and about saying 'no' to unilateral disarmament. The research indicated that members were in favour of a wealth tax, of a move against private schools by removing their tax advantages and in favour of employees in the boardrooms. Although members wished to limit trade union immunities and do away with the closed shop, they saw themselves as belonging to a reforming party. They also wanted Roy Jenkins as leader.

This research, based on answers from a substantial 8% of the membership, was reassuring to politicians coming mainly from a divided Labour Party. The SDP was a unique mix of experienced professional politicians and a membership largely comprising people who had never previously joined any political party. The Refugees and the Naives, as the two types became popularly known, were in step.

In the nine months since its birth, the SDP had moved forward almost without interruption. Continued success in the immediate future seemd likely.

Yet Social Democrats, though elated, were not counting their chickens. As the emergent new party of conscience and reform, would the SDP replace Labour as the major party of the left?

CONCLUSION:

WHAT FUTURE
THE PROGRESSIVE LEFT?

WHAT FUTURE THE PROGRESSIVE LEFT?

To anyone following the fortunes of the Labour Party, a simple pattern becomes obvious: fifty years up, thirty years down. The first fifty years show growing support, leading through minority Labour Governments to the post-war summit of Labour achievement. For the next thirty years the Party drifts downwards, with electoral support inexorably ebbing away. By 1979 Labour's share of the vote was smaller than in 1929.

For those subscribing to the historical theory of inevitability, it may be tempting to conclude that the Labour Party has come to the end of the road, that it is doomed now to wither. Perhaps like an ageing Hollywood star, it may make a come-back or two, but its days of glory are just a nostalgic memory. The future of the Social Democratic Party will be determined by the validity of this theory.

But inevitability is often elusive. For example, those in the Labour Party who have had visions that a new compassionate society must inevitably replace the uncaring profit-motivated capitalist Britain are still waiting. Indeed they must have been more than surprised that the swing was going the other way, that the Tory Party should have won the 1979 General Election so convincingly, with considerable support from working people.

Likewise, the Kremlin must have been disappointed over the years with the elusiveness of its inevitable world domination. For even as it held on to Eastern Europe, its influence in the world was not the inexorable forward march it wished. It lost as many battles as it won, including Yugoslavia, China, Albania, Egypt, and had its share of problems with Hungary, Czechoslovakia, Romania and Poland.

How inevitable is Labour's demise today? What future is there for the SDP? The two questions go together. However, they require a split answer: short-term, as far as the next election in 1983/4, and thereafter.

The Next Election: Who Will Win?

The Alliance has broken through the 'wasted vote' barrier. More or less from the start, it led the political field: in opinion polls, council and parliamentary by-elections. The consistency of the results was extraordinary. Support for the Alliance grew, and stabilised at around 40 to 50%: Warrington 42.4%; Croydon North West 40%; GLC St Pancras 43.6%; Crosby 49.1%.

Perhaps the most accurate indication of the underlying trend came from the council by-elections. By the end of 1981, the Alliance was winning no less than two out of three council by-elections, while Labour was losing two out of three. This astonishing pattern was on a vote of 46% for the Alliance, with Labour gaining 27% and the Conservatives 25%, according to a *New Statesman* analysis in December 1981.

The people were giving this verdict nationwide, obliterating normal voting patterns, obliterating discrepancies between North and South, town and country, Labour and Conservative.

This voting pattern, if repeated at the next General Election, would mean Alliance victory and government. But almost unbelievably, due to the idiosyncratic electoral system, results to date still only bring the Alliance to the margin of victory.

The eccentricity of the electoral system and the danger of firm forecasts were highlighted by David Butler in the *Sunday Times* of 8 November 1981. Butler's analysis, itself based on work done by Clive Payne of Oxford University's social studies computer unit, confirms that to achieve victory the Alliance must win a considerably higher percentage of votes than either Labour or Conservatives. Indeed, Labour, through its high concentrations of support, starts with a built-in advantage over both the Conservatives and the Alliance. Nothing proves this more starkly than Butler's example of what happens when each party gains precisely one third of the votes: Labour wins 290 seats, the Conservatives 260 and the Alliance only 79.

Butler's forecast considers other possible permutations; it shows that each party's result is determined not only by its own vote but by the split in the vote across the other two parties. In a three-party national contest a party's fortune can move "extraordinarily fast from famine to feast" or from feast to famine, as can be seen from Butler's statistics below.

*The first table below shows the various shares of the popular
vote likely to produce five different election results, the second,
how the number of seats won by the major parties can be
altered dramatically by small percentage changes in the
popular vote*

	Con	Lab	SDP/Lib	Ireland
1 Conservative working majority				
Major party vote (GB)	39%	33%	28%	—
Seats	332	263	34	17
2 Labour working majority				
Major party vote (GB)	31%	36%	33%	—
Seats	214	332	83	17
3 Alliance working majority				
Major party vote (GB)	33%	25%	42%	—
Seats	126	171	332	17
4 Con-Lab deadlock				
Major party vote (GB)	36%	35%	29%	—
Seats	291	296	42	17
5 Three-way split				
Major party vote (GB)	34%	27%	39%	—
Seats	233	222	174	17

Major party vote and seats won

Con	32%	217
Lab	32%	295
Alliance	36%	117

Con	31%	169
Lab	31%	288
Alliance	38%	172

Con	30%	96
Lab	30%	257
Alliance	40%	276

Con	29%	39
Lab	29%	226
Alliance	42%	364

Con	28%	13
Lab	28%	187
Alliance	44%	429

Furthermore, the Alliance begins to win seats disproportionately beyond a certain point. For two percentage points it can win an additional one hundred or so seats; 4% more votes can mean 30% more representation and the prize of government, with 42% or 364 seats in the House of Commons.

Conversely, before that breakthrough is reached, it is Labour which is positively helped by the existence of the SDP Alliance. Thus *example 2* shows Labour with 36%, or 1% fewer votes than in the decisive defeat of 1979, this time able to form a government with a clear majority.

Thus, in December 1981 Labour was still within reach of victory, as under certain circumstances were the Conservatives. The 1984 election was not quite in the bag yet. Much would depend on the actual split of votes and the run-up period to the General Election.

But clearly the tide of opinion was going the Alliance's way. When David Steel addressed the Liberal Conference and said: "Prepare for government", this was no fanciful way of speaking. The long slog of a holding campaign was over. Warrington was the El Alamein of the campaign. The morale of the troops was high. They could smell victory. The psychological advantage over the opposing parties in a state of retreat and even of chaos was real.

The Alliance may still suffer setbacks. It would be surprising if nothing went amiss. Considerable scope still exists for discord between the SDP and Liberals, as was seen in the carving-up of the constituencies. The choice of an SDP leader, and the basis on which he or she is elected, is fertile soil for public argument. Doubtless SDP spokesmen will occasionally hit the headlines with gaffes made and bricks dropped. But for any of that to be an impediment of substance is unlikely. The momentum of the Alliance is too great for that.

For the same reason, the old argument that by-election victories in mid-term have no significance is largely discounted both by the size and the consistency of the swings to the Alliance. The question is not whether a constituency is regained susbsequently, but what the trend of by-election swings signifies.

Where in the past there has been a trend, contrary to conventional wisdom, this has proved to be meaningful. Thus, half a dozen Labour by-election victories between 1962 and 1964 heralded the Labour victory of 1964; the Conservative by-election victories between 1967 and 1969 under Wilson were followed by a Tory government; the six Tory by-election gains from 1975 to 1978 served as introduction to the Thatcher government; and the five Liberal gains in 1972 to 1973, though they could not usher in a Liberal government, proved to be the curtain-raiser to a near tripling of Liberal votes.

Whatever Labour and Tories do between now and 1984 would seem unlikely to change the political trend favouring the Alliance either sufficiently or in time. The Conservatives are trapped by their policy, Labour by its divisions.

Mid-way through its term of office, the Conservative Government has little choice but to continue with its tough monetarist policy. Having consistently proclaimed that there is no alterntive, to alter course would scarcely reap electoral benefits. First, it would be perceived as a U-turn, and would be interpreted either as acknowledgement that the policy had failed, or as a cynical self-seeking move to help win the election. Second, a move away from strict monetarism would in any case not solve the problem of three million unemployed quickly enough.

Yet unemployment is the overriding issue which concerns the electorate. This was as evident in July 1981, at the Warrington by-election, as it was six months later. However, this is the very issue which the Government cannot solve in the time available - at most two-and-a-half years. For, as Employment Secretary Norman Tebbit points out, throwing money at unemployment will not make it go away. The expenditure of billions of pounds would, by 1984, not reduce unemployment below two and a half million people, and would destroy both the Government's anti-inflationary policy and its credibility.

The problem is compounded for the Government and for Mrs Thatcher. Both suffer from an uncaring image, the former being associated with record unemployment figures in the thirties, and the latter with a cold personal style seemingly lacking in compassion. Due to the lack of success of its economic policies, the Government is less popular than it has ever been. Yet there is little it can do to win more support before 1984.

The Labour Party, for its part, is trapped by its situation. It may try to prepare for the elections - witness the meeting convened by the trade unions at Bishop's Stortford in January 1982, with David Basnett proclaiming that "Peace has broken out in the Labour Party" - but the divisions do not disappear. Within hours the peace was in question. For peace was on the Left's terms, Tony Benn indicating he would not contest the deputy leadership in 1982, if the Party desisted from expelling extremists. Left-wing policies would continue as before. So would re-selection of MPs. The Left's gains were not to be challenged by the Right.

Labour moderates immediately questioned the terms of the peace. The underlying problem remained: to accept left-wing extremism or to fight it and exacerbate party divisions. Either way was to jeopardise Labour's electoral prospects. The Party's fundamental problem was as before: a deeply divided party could scarcely expect to win the electorate's trust.

The political reality is that neither major party is able to change its immediate destiny. Both are experiencing unprecedented problems which they have brought upon themselves. Whatever changes can be effected in the short-term are not enough. King Canute's single-mindedness of purpose would seem insufficient to stem the incoming tide of the Alliance, a single-mindedness demonstrably lacking in this case.

Those who argue that Alliance support will drop before the next General Election must surely be right. The question is at what point does support drop, from what peak will the downward consolidation begin? The statistics of Butler's analysis clearly indicate that this is crucial.

Yet given the evidence available, the likeliest scenario is that the Alliance wins the 1984 election outright. Failing that, it should win enough seats to be in the government as partner in a coalition.

In one important respect, the Alliance grouping is like Communism: once in power, it is in for ever. But where Communism does this by abolishing elections and installing a dictatorship of the proletariat, the Alliance would achieve permanent government through the introduction of proportional representation. For under proportional representation, the party of the centre is almost guaranteed a place in government.

The outcome of elections based on proportional representation would most often be a coalition government. Rarely would a single party win over 50% of the votes, enabling it to be the sole party in government. In a three-party situation, the party of the centre must normally join with one of the 'outer' parties to form the coalition, as is the case in Germany. During the seventies in Britain, for example, proportional representation would have meant continuous coalition government, with Liberal participation. Thus even if the SDP Alliance is not the majority party, its inclusion in government would normally be assured.

Although proportional representation has not in the past suited Labour or Tories, their attitudes are likely to be different in the future. For it may actually benefit the older parties more than the SDP/Liberal Alliance. In a situation where it is winning 45% of the votes the Alliance could, under the present system, win nearly five hundred seats. The Tories, with 25% of the vote or less, could be obliterated, ending up with a dozen or so MPs. In such circumstances, the Tories might well prefer proportional representation and the safety net of 150/160 seats to hovering on the brink of annihilation. The same could be true for Labour.

In 1983/4, the SDP Alliance should win, and introduce proportional representation. Proportional representation will, above all, be fair and democracy will be seen to be working. Government will reflect the electorate's intentions.

Beyond 1984

When Labour and Conservative politicians scoff at the Social Democrats, they do so with good reason. The existence of their parties is threatened. Labour spokesmen refer to the

SDP as an alternative Tory party. Conservatives see the Social Democrats as socialists. They cannot both be right, but according to which thesis is more accurate, one of the two parties is more threatened. Either, as Gerald Kaufman says, the Tories are suffering a terminal illness and will be replaced by the new Tories, or Labour is dying and will be replaced by the new socialists.

The SDP is what it calls itself: a party of conscience and reform. It has been launched by former Labour ministers. Its MPs have nearly all come from Labour. Its entire heritage is progressive, reforming. To call it Tory is a misrepresentation either wilful or eccentric. If it is a direct competitor to one of the major parties it must surely be to Labour. The SDP Alliance will replace Labour as the major representative of left-wing progressive reform. But proportional representation will ensure that all three parties continue to co-exist.

If the Conservatives are at risk, this is mainly in the one forthcoming election under the present electoral system. The Conservative Party has the resilience to come bouncing back. The Thatcher victory itself was an example of a remarkable come-back, with an increase of over eight percentage points with 13.7 million people voting Conservative, only marginally less than the post-war record Conservative votes of 1951 and 1959.

If Thatcherite Conservatism has since proved less than popular, this unpopularity is because it is a deviation from the norm and not the norm itself. Toryism has been characterised by common sense, adapting to events, bowing to the wind like the proverbial reed which does not snap. This Tory government has been the exception. It has made an economic goal its only goal. It has adopted dogma and worship of one economic creed, refusing to adapt to economic and social pressures. In due course Conservatism will return to its normal path, shedding dogma on the way. Thatcherism will be seen as an historic aberration.

Of Conservative MPs only Christopher Brocklebank-Fowler has so far joined the Social Democrats, although one or two lesser Tories have crossed over. Edward Heath spoke about possibly joining in a coalition, but added that there was no question of membership of the new party so long as it retained its socialist credentials. The dissatisfaction in Conservative ranks is temporary and runs less deep than Labour disillusion.

The Conservatives are conservative with a small 'c', as

are millions of British people. There is something in the
Conservative proposition which has and will continue to find
an echo in the nation's character: "Let's carry on as we are.
Better the devil you know. Don't stir things. Leave it in the
hands of the Tories. They know what they are doing."
Conservative government (though not the Thatcher
experiment) is synonymous with effective government. The
Disraeli 'one nation' philosophy, tempered and brought into
the twentieth century by the reforming attitudes of politicians
like Butler, Macmillan and Macleod, ensures a place for
undogmatic Conservatism in British politics.

There is a place for a party which represents the
merchant interests of the shopkeepers in the High Street, the
engineering works managers on the industrial estate, and the
accountants and bankers in the City.

The Labour Party, on the other hand, has been following
its chosen path consistently over a long period, playing the
role for which it has become well-known. It is *because* it is
acting in character that its future is at risk. The pattern of
decline must not only continue, but will inevitably accelerate
due to the new competition of the Alliance. There is something
dramatically amiss for the main opposition party not to profit
from the Tory Government's problem of three million
unemployed. The electors of Warrington, Croydon and Crosby
registered a vote of No Confidence in Labour as well as in
Conservatives.

Labour's champions will claim there is time for recovery.
All that needs be done is to unite and present the Party's
policies to the electorate. However, even more important is the
question of trust. Will voters buy their car from the Labour
garage?

In a party where Michael Foot and Neil Kinnock are the
moderates, where part of the right wing has left and more will
follow into the SDP, and where the PLP, the last bastion of the
right, is to become predominantly cf the left during the
eighties, all the meaningful pressures are still left-wing. The
Hattersleys and the Healeys, as long as they remain in the
Party, will serve as a reminder of former times rather than
have a significant role to play. For the Labour Party, the
Social Democratic Mark II option is no longer on offer. Nor is
the Broad Church party on offer.

Because the Labour Left must triumph, Labour is fated
to become the minor of two progressive parties. For a future
Labour Party of the left is committed to the very aspects

which have been losing it support in the past. Its appeal has been too narrow and will become more narrow in the future. A number of ingredients contribute to that.

As long ago as 1959, Gaitskell saw the problem of Labour's restricted vision. He wanted to move away from a strictly working-class appeal. The Party rejected his advice and support declined for two decades. Today, the Party is still committed to a narrow concept, but it is considerably weaker and the political competition is stronger. Left-wing guru Professor Eric Hobsbawm, also sees this as the problem. In *The Forward March of Labour Halted?**, he suggests that the forward march can only be resumed by "parties that have moved forward not *only* as class parties, and still less as sectional pressure groups and alliances of minority interests, but as 'people's parties' with which the majority of their nation interested in progressive reform and change can identify; as spokesman for the nation in time of crisis."

But people's parties do depend on a broad spectrum of people. "I do not suppose" writes Hobsbawm, "that the loss of Roy Jenkins as a person was much regretted. But it is a mistake to dismiss the collective secession of the Social Democrats and the foundation of a new party as good riddance. It represents the loss of a significant section of the left-of-centre middle class, which long looked to Labour." But even more relevant to the prospects of the Labour Party are those outside the Party, the voters, for, says Hobsbawm, "The future of Labour and the advance to socialism depends on mobilizing people who remember the date of the Beatles' break-up and not the date of the Saltley pickets: of people who have never read *Tribune* and who do not care a damn about the deputy-leadership of the Labour Party. ... The future depends on men and women, blue-collar, white-collar and no collar, ranging from zero CSE to PhD, who are, regrettably, not revolutionaries, even though they want a new and better Britain."

In that last statement of Hobsbawm's lies the clue perhaps to Labour's built-in difficulty: the mismatch between the dedicated vision of the activist and the interests of normal people. The party activist wants a revolution of the system, whilst the voter wants improvements, a better deal but not the dogma of a socialist society. There is the inherent paradox of a

---

* Published in association with *Marxism Today* by Verso Editions, 1981

movement which is intent on handing down what is best for the working man: the paradox of the party hierarchy, of an elite handing down socialism, the brotherhood of man. How do you impose Utopia?

The Labour Party's prescription in the 1980s will continue to include ingredients long since discredited. Careful presentation to the public will not help.

The patient has to have confidence in both the medicine and the doctor; and having tried both over many years and having found them wanting, he is unlikely to ask the same doctor for more of the same medicine: nationalisation and the trade union connection.

As in Gaitskell's day, nationalisation is Labour's sacred cow. In 1959, the issue could be left on the shelf to collect dust. Over the years it has become increasingly important.

The electorate has consistently indicated that it thought nationalisation at best irrelevant, at worst harmful to the economy. Only the small percentage of the committed believe it to be the crucial lynchpin of future economic development to benefit the whole of the working population rather than shareholders only.

Yet to a pragmatic population, what benefit nationalised industry? Has owning one's own coal, gas, ships, or airlines raised the standard of living? Has diverting profits from shareholders to all added one penny to wage packets? Have Russian or Romanian factory workers benefited from being the owners of their industries? Is their standard of living higher than that of the English or Norwegians? Yet total nationalisation, East-European style, is the prize at the end of the Labour Party road. Nationalised industries are not seen as efficient either. Where Marks and Spencer impresses, the local Gas Board depresses.

To nationalise as a matter of fundamental policy avoids the underlying problem of the economy. Nor does it, *per se*, make the country richer; nor does it inspire international confidence; nor does it improve the lot of the working man. To nationalise according to the merits of individual cases would be different, but that is to stray onto Social Democratic beliefs. At best, national debates about nationalisation distract from the real issues: just as the Debate about the merits of remaining in the EEC was a misuse of the country's time, so continued discussions on further nationalisation are irrelevant to the country's real problems. To quote David Marquand: "Labour Governments of the seventies wasted

201

huge quantities of legislative time and energy on totally unnecessary extensions of public ownership in the shipbuilding and aircraft industries and in the docks." To vote Labour in the eighties is to choose more nationalisation. Labour is irreversibly committed to it.

As in Gaitskell's time so in the eighties nationalisation as a dogmatic belief is based on a misconception. It will drive voters away, now as then. It marks the party as both old-fashioned and lacking in judgement. It makes the broad electorate sceptical about the Labour Party's ability to run the nation's affairs.

The Labour Party's trade union connection and the insistence on a special relationship does it electoral harm. The trade unions' image, according to successive opinion polls, is bad. Unions are seen as careless of the interests of those affected by their industrial actions. Their earlier image of fighters for the underprivileged has all but vanished. The Labour movement is tarred with the trade union brush.

As left-wing academic Raymond Williams writes in his contribution to *The Forward March of Labour Halted?*: "the most shattering fact in our culture is that not only the employers and the rich and their friends and agents believe and say that we are all interested only in selfish advantage: a majority in our society believe and say this, including a large and growing number, cynically or angrily, within our own organisations."*

Large numbers of trade unionists are not Labour sympathisers. A third of them voted Conservative at the 1979 election. Half the skilled workers voted Conservative. Nearly three-quarters of the ASTMS white collar union opt out of paying the political levy to the Labour Party. Half the trade unions are not affiliated to the Labour Party.

So the Labour Party is saddled with the worst of both worlds: a trade union institution unpopular with the electorate and even unpopular with its members. The trade unions are seen as a barrier to effective government.

The Labour Party is committed to its left-wing role. Ideology has in the past, and must in the future, dominate Labour Party thinking, involving violent theological disputes, all the more violent if the Right is still represented within the Party. Divisions and bitter strife must continue to be the lot of

---

* Eric Hobsbawm and others, Verso Editions, 1981

a left-dominated Labour Party.

The Party is committed to its vision of a class-dominated society: Labour's continuing mission will be to represent the interests of the working classes, thus exacerbating society's divisions. Waging a class war outside, and continuing to do battle inside, the Labour Party will increasingly be seen as a narrow-based, and to many a narrow-minded, party. It will be seen as such by more and more people in an ever-wider consumer society, in Hobsbawm's regrettably not revolutionary Britain of blue-collars, white-collars and no collars.

It cannot any longer become a people's party, a *Volkspartei* after the Brandt and Schmidt prototype, and is therefore destined to a diminishing role. Unless the present electoral system allows the party to slip into power in 1983/84, on yet another record low vote - an unlikely prospect - a second chance of power is unlikely to recur. At best, under a new system of proportional representation, Labour can hope to be a junior partner in coalitions. It can scarcely expect to form government. Its role may still have significance in the long term. It may yet develop the role of conscience of the nation, a ginger group of the broad Left. Its contributions to the nation's affairs can again become important. It can, however, no longer be central.

The Labour Party will thus have emerged as a Party of the far left, its characteristics more clearly defined. Tony Benn will, barring accidents, emerge properly as its leader. It will have a very strong appeal for those who identify with it. But it will have that appeal for fewer people. It will become the left-wing rump of the progressive movement in Great Britain. The electorate will have a clear choice of left-wing parties - between the new, sharply-defined Labour Party of the left and the progressive party of conscience and reform, the people's party, the SDP.

The New People's Party

The SDP Alliance may well win the next election. But to win a second and subsequent elections it will need to prove itself. The future of the Alliance and its success as a government will depend on three factors: first, SDP and Liberals must decide on their long-term relationship; second, the Alliance must establish a sound working relationship with the unions; last, the Alliance must prove that people's faith in it is justified.

The future of the Alliance itself will be one of the first questions to resolve. Within the SDP and Liberal parties different views are held, advocating variously a merger of the two parties, a retention of separate identities within one Alliance, and total separation after the introduction of proportional representation. The last is attractive both to some Social Democrats, for example David Owen, and to those Liberals jealous of their party's separate identity.

Yet for the SDP and the Liberals to part company would be neither in their best interest nor in the interest of those who voted for Alliance government. The electorate might well view an arrangement lasting for one election as a breach of faith, more in keeping with the old two-party spirit of adversary politics.

For the majority, both within the Alliance and amongst the electorate, the attraction of the partnership is that little separates the two parties, that they pursue almost identical policies, that it is not merely a marriage of convenience but is, in the words of Roy Jenkins, a partnership of principle. Although a minority disagrees, this is most likely to continue. "The Alliance must be permanent", wrote Dick Taverne in *The Times* (12 January 1982).

All things being equal, a Social Democratic leader will emerge as the head of the Alliance. Present indications are that that person will be Roy Jenkins. Should the Liberals become the larger of the two parties in the House of Commons, David Steel could emerge as the leader. However, the Alliance would in all important respects be the same, whether led by Jenkins or by Steel. The views of the two men are so similar and their relationship so good, that the two working in tandem, regardless of who is the leader, would not materially affect the type of leadership. However, Steel, who is still in his early forties, is more likely to succeed Jenkins at a later date. He is respected by the Gang of Four and by those who work with him, and opinion polls show that he is held in high esteem by the public.

Long-term, the Alliance will be judged by its ability to arrest national decline. Alternate Labour and Conservative governments have failed to do so. If the Alliance also fails, the country has exhausted the available options. According to some political observers, democracy itself could come under threat through more extreme regimes of Right or Left.

In the past twenty years, the unions have brought down three governments, destroyed five incomes policies and so far

defeated two initiatives to curb their power. The SDP Alliance
must fare better if it is to succeed. But why should it?

The fundamental situation may change. It may be in the
interest of the unions to co-operate with the Alliance. If the
Labour Party becomes the smaller of the two progressive
parties, and its natural support stabilises at, say, 20% of the
vote, it would never be able to form a government again. At
best, it could be the junior partner in a coalition.

If the Labour Party can no longer deliver, how long
before the trade union movement adapts to the new reality?
The TUC may have created the Labour Party and recently
strengthened its links with it, but trade unionists are realists.
On the Continent, good working relationships exist between
unions and different political parties, and they existed here in
the post-war period. Though such a development would
initially be resisted, the unions would inevitably begin to move
away from their exclusive relationship with the Labour Party
and explore links with the Alliance.

At the same time, the Alliance would have considerable
scope to encourage co-operation within the membership. A
sizeable percentage of trade unionists are neither members of
the Labour Party nor vote for it. According to a MORI poll
carried out on behalf of Granada's Television programme,
World in Action, and reported by *The Times* of 19 January
1982, 56% believe that their union should not be affiliated to
the Labour Party, 45% feel that the Labour Party no longer
represents the interests of working people, 36% declared they
would vote for the SDP Alliance if a general election were held
tomorrow.

Given the new situation of a union movement which sees
its own interest moving away from exclusive links with the
Labour Party, the SDP's ideas may fall on more fertile soil. In
the past, Bill Rodgers' advocacy of a loosening of the ties
between unions and the Labour Party has understandably met
with hostility. At present 90% of Labour Party finance comes
from the unions; each unionist pays a political levy to the
Party unless he specifically contracts out. Rodgers proposes
that members should pay only by specifically contracting in
and, more important, should pay to the party of their choice.
The Labour Party would be compensated for the resulting loss
of half its finances through a new system of state funding of
political parties.

A strong historic link would be exchanged for greater
freedom: the Labour Party would be independent of trade

union money. The unions would emerge free to pursue their own interests, to work constructively with the government of the day.

Clearly this whole process of change, in spite of the more favourable circumstances, will be fought by hard-core Labour and Communist unionists. The SDP Alliance, unlike a Conservative government, is, however, in a better position to encourage change through its own credentials as an offspring of the Labour movement. By encouraging democratic procedures - through the greater use of the secret ballot, for example - it can help make unions genuinely representative rather than allow control by extremist groups whose interests are opposed to those of government.

The SPD Alliance must run the country efficiently, yet look after the disadvantaged. It needs to be a government of compassionate materialism or, in SDP terminology, market socialism. Two out of every five people now support the SDP Alliance and that is likely to be its natural level of support. In the final analysis, however, the proof of the pudding is in the eating. If the SDP in government achieves what it seems to promise, it will continue to win elections. The Alliance's own efforts will determine whether it becomes the people's party of the next twenty years.

CHRONOLOGY

MAIN EVENTS LEADING UP TO THE BIRTH OF THE SOCIAL DEMOCRATIC PARTY

27/28 February 1900 Birth of the Labour Party, initially known as the Labour Representation Committee

November 1959 Labour Party Clause 4 debate. Gaitskell fails to gain acceptance to modernise Party. Labour to remain a working-class party of narrow appeal

November 1959 Social Democratic Party of Germany (SPD) agrees to become a national party with broad appeal, according to the Bad Godesberg Programme

October 1960 Gaitskell's "Fight and fight and fight" speech; Labour leadership defeated on issue of unilateral nuclear disarmament

October 1960 Campaign for Democratic Socialism launched to mobilise Labour's right wing

October 1961 Unilateralists decisively beaten. Victory for the Right

28 October 1971 Roy Jenkins and 68 Labour rebels vote with Conservative government to take Britain into the Common Market

1 March 1973 Dick Taverne wins by-election as Democratic Labour candidate

5 June 1975 Referendum keeps Britain in the Common Market

October 1979 Labour annual conference agrees compulsory re-selection procedure for MPs

November 1979 Roy Jenkins makes 'Dimbleby' speech, arguing for a re-alignment in British politics

November 1979 Bill Rodgers makes Abertillery speech saying that Labour has one year to put its house in order

May 1980 Campaign for Labour Victory conference at Birmingham. Labour Party members discuss leaving the Party

June 1980 Jenkins' speech to Parliamentary Press Club

1 August 1980 Gang of Three's letter in the *Guardian* discusses "acceptable socialist alternative"

October 1980 Labour annual conference agrees principle of electoral college to elect party leader and deputy leader

6 January 1981 Roy Jenkins returns from Brussels

24 January 1981 Special Labour Party conference votes for composition of electoral college for electing party leader: 40% trade unions, 30% PLP, 30% CLPs

25 January 1981 Limehouse Declaration bringing into existence Council for Social Democracy

THE SDP'S FIRST YEAR

16 June 'A Fresh Start for Britain': SDP/Liberal partnership agreed in principle

16 July Warrington by-election. Jenkins loses

September Liberal Assembly approves SDP/Liberal Alliance by 1,600 votes to 112

22 October Croydon North West by-election won by Bill Pitt, Liberal, as first Alliance MP to be elected

26 November Crosby by-election. Shirley Williams becomes first elected SDP MP

31 December 1981 ends with 27 SDP and 12 Liberal MPs in House of Commons

RESEARCH SOURCES

RESEARCH SOURCES

The research for this book consisted of interviews with the people acknowledged in the introduction, as well as a study of books, journals, newspapers and other published material spanning eighty years, of which the more important are listed below.

BOOKS

Birdsey, Min, *A Pictorial History of the Labour Party 1900-1975*, publishers, The Labour Party, 1975

Butler, David, and **Sloman**, Anne, *British Political Facts 1900-1979*, Macmillan, 1980

Cook, Chris, *A Short History of the Liberal Party 1900-1976*, Macmillan, 1980

Cormack, Patrick (Editor), *Right Turn*, Leo Cooper, 1978

Crosland, Anthony, *The Future of Socialism*, Jonathan Cape, 1956

Finer, S E, *The Changing British Party System 1945-1979*, American Institute for Public Policy Research, 1980

Haseler, Stephen,
The Gaitskellites, Macmillan, 1969
The Death of British Democracy, Paul Elek, 1976
The Tragedy of Labour, Blackwell, 1980

Hobsbawm, Eric, and others, *The Forward March of Labour Halted?*, Verso, 1981

Howell, David, *British Social Democracy*, 1980

Kaufman, Gerald (Editor), *The Left*, Anthony Blond, 1966

Miliband, Ralph, *Marxism and Politics*, OUP, 1977

Milligan, Stephen, *The New Barons*, Temple Smith, 1976

Owen, David, *Face the Future*, Jonathan Cape, 1981

Pelling, Henry, *Short History of the Labour Party*, Macmillan, 1968

Rogaly, Joe, *Parliament for the People - A Handbook of Electoral Reform*, Temple Smith, 1976

Roth, Andrew, *The MPs' Chart, Parliamentary Profiles*, 1980

Sked, Alan, and **Cook**, Chris, *Post-War Britain*, Penguin, 1980

Spanier, *Europe our Europe*, Secker & Warburg, 1972

Stewart, Margaret, *Protest or Power?*, Allen & Unwin, 1974

Taverne, Dick, *The Future of the Left*, Jonathan Cape, 1974

Williams, Shirley, *Politics is for People*, Penguin, 1981

Windlesham, Lord, *Communication and Political Power*, Jonathan Cape, 1966

ARTICLES AND PAMPHLETS

Bealey, Frank, 'Negotiations between the Liberals and the LRC before the 1906 election', from *Bulletin of the Institute of Historical Research*, XXIX 1956

Benn, Tony, 'The Case for Party Democracy', The Labour Party, 1980

Campaign for Labour Party Victory, 'The Future of the Labour Party', 1980

Mullin, Chris, 'How to Select or Reselect Your MP', Campaign for Labour Party Democracy & The Institute for Workers' Control, 1981

Nairn, Tom, 'The Nature of the Labour Party', *New Left Review*, May-June 1964

Sozialdemokratische Partei Deutschlands, 'Grundsatzprogramm der SPD', Bad Godesberg Programme, Special Conference of the SPD, 13-15 November, 1959

Tribune Group, 'Labour - Party or Puppet?', 1972

Underhill, Reg, 'Underhill Report on the Militant Tendency', 1980

NEWSPAPERS AND JOURNALS

Newspaper and journal comment has been a rich vein of information and entertainment. I have drawn mostly from the following:

The Times, The Guardian, The New Statesman, The Sunday Times, Tribune, The Observer, The Daily Mail, The Daily Express, The Daily Sketch, The Sun, The Daily Telegraph, The Financial Times, The Listener, The Daily Mirror

I am also indebted to opinion polls taken by Gallup, National Opinion Polls (NOP), Market & Opinion Research International (MORI).

INDEX

Benn, Tony, 44, 89, 90, 122; in Labour cabinet, 78, 122-3; left-wing campaign, 69, 106, 119-21, 159-60, 203; 1980 deputy leadership campaign, 119-20, 159-62

Bevan, Aneurin, 35, 36, 41, 49

Butskellism, 34-5, R A Butler, 101

By-elections, Parliamentary, significance of results, 93-5, 172, 195; 1962-4, 94, 95, 195; 1967-9, 195; 1970-4, 94-5, 172, 195; 1974-9, 94, 195; Alliance participation, Warrington, 13, 14, 22, 155, 165, 166-73, results of, 171, 178; Croydon North West, 95-6, 173, 178, 183; Crosby, 178, 183

Callaghan, James, in Wilson Cabinet, 61, 64, 65, 68, 80, 82; leadership election 1976, 118; as Labour Party Leader, 22, 36, 72, 75, 95, 99, 104-5, 106, 123-4, 126, 138, 142, 144

CDS (Campaign for Democratic Socialism), 23, 39, 44-5, 51-55, 110

CLV (Campaign for Labour Victory), 54, formation and membership, 110; activities, 127; influence on formation of SDP, 127-30; Birmingham conference 1980, 134-5, 145; Highbury conference, 146

CND (Campaign for Nuclear Disarmament), 9, 48, 97-8

CSD (Campaign for Social Democracy), *see* **Taverne, Dick**

Castle, Barbara, 41, 63, 66, 78

Cocks, Michael, Chief Whip, dispute with Benn, 123

Common Market, *see* **Labour Party**, EEC issue

Conservative Party, defectors to SDP, 12, 184, 198; electoral decline, 92-6; future of, 198-9; leaders, Douglas-Home, Alec, 59; Macmillan, Harold, 40, 59; Heath, Edward, 7, 66, 76, 79, 82, 84, 95, 107; Thatcher, Margaret, 7, 11, 22, 38, 44, 76, 157-8, 184, 195-6, 198-9

Council for Social Democracy, 5, 48, 119, 157 (*see also* **SDP**, creation)

Crick, Professor Bernard, 63, 131

Crosland, Anthony, *see* Socialism, CDS

Daly, Jim, 2, 132-3, 134-5, 147, 175; and Radical Centre, 132-3

Defectors, *see* Labour Party, Conservative Party

Democratic Labour, *see* Taverne, Dick

Dimbleby Lecture, 130-2 (*see also* Jenkins, Roy)

EEC, *see* Labour Party, EEC issue

Elections (*see also* By-elections)
General: 1929, 17; 1959, 38; 1964, 53, 59, 63; 1966, 63; Feb 1974, 6, 7, 17, 69, 70, 72, 73, 86, 89-90, 96; May 1979, 6, 7, 13, 191; May 1981 council elections, 157, 179; GLC by-elections, 156; Council by-elections, 12, 184, 192

Electoral Predictions, David Butler, 192-4, 196

Electoral System, criticism of, 6, 91-2; case for reform, 1, 8, 16, 17, 93-4, 96-7, 197, 198, 203

Entryism, *see* Labour Party, Far Left

Fabian Society, 32, 33 (*see also* Labour Party, origins)

Foot, Michael, 83, 87, 108, 123, 126, 199; in Wilson Cabinet, 73-4; leadership elections, 1976, 118; 1980, 118, 138, 158; as Labour Party leader, 119, 158-64, 167; attitude to Far Left, 186

Gaitskell, Hugh, 28, 34, 52-4, 61, 62, 66, 78, 86; modernisation of Party, 30, 39-50, 200-2; and Liberals, 180

Gang of Three/Four, *see* SDP, Jenkins, Roy, Owen, David, Rodgers, Bill, Williams, Shirley

Hattersley, Roy, 28, 84, 106, 128-9, 158, 160, 162, 163

Healey, Denis, in Wilson Cabinet, 65, 75, 102; under Callaghan, 106, 123-4, 158; leadership election, 138-9, 162, 185

Heath, Edward, *see* Conservative Party, leaders

Hobsbawm, Eric, 200-1

220

Houghton Committee, *see* **Labour Party**, historic decline

Hoyle, Douglas, *see* **By-elections**, Warrington

ILP (Independent Labour Party), *see* **Labour Party**, origins

Industrial Relations Act, 72-3, 79; 1974 repeal of, 74

Jay, Douglas, 39, 52, 78

Jenkins, Roy, 77, 200; role in Labour Government, 65, 80, 81, 83-5, 111, 123; and Taverne, 87-8, 90; appointment to EEC Commission, 90, 111; Dimbleby Lecture, 130-2, 175; return from Brussels, 5, 147; run-up to SDP, 137, 145, 147, 175-6; Warrington, 129, 166-73, 178, 183; as possible leader, 21-2, 187, 204

LCC (Labour Coordinating Committee), *see* **Labour Party**, left-wing campaign

Labour Party, conferences: Blackpool 1959, 40-4; Scarborough 1960, 46-8, 52, 86; Blackpool 1961, 53; Brighton 1962, 78; 1968, 65-6; Annual 1970, 80; Special 1970, 80; Brighton 1971, 82; Special 1971, 80; Brighton 1979, 126; Blackpool 1980, 122, 140, 142-5; Wembley, Special, 1980, 118-9, 135-6; Wembley, Special, January 1981, 5, 48, 119-20, 127, 147; Brighton 1981, 185

defectors to SDP: 12-3, 77, 100, 110-2, 125, 153, 156; Aylestone, Lord (Herbert Bowden), 13; Bradley, Tom, 12, 81; Bullock, Lord, 13; Cartwright, John, 12, 110, 113, 140-2; Crawshaw, Richard, 13; Diamond, Lord, 2, 13, 82; Dickson Mabon, Dr John, 84, 179; Donaldson, Lord, 13; Ellis, Tom, 12, 140-2; Harris, Lord, 13, 133, 147; Horam, John, 2, 12, 125, 126, 127, 133, 137, 140-2; Hunt, Lord, 13; Kennet, Lord, 13; Lyons, Edward, 12; Maclennan, Robert, 2, 12, 90; Marquand, David, *see separate entry*; Perry, Lord, 13; Roper, John, 12, 140-2; Walston, Lord, 13; Weidenfeld, Lord, 13; Wellbeloved, Jim, 13; Winterbottom, Lord, 13; Wrigglesworth, Ian, 12, 110, 140-2; Young, Lord, 13;

defectors to Liberal Party: Mayhew, Christopher, 100, 111, 112

defectors to Conservative

Party: Prentice, Reg, 73, 111, 112-3
defence policy, 35, 37, 39, 44-7, 52-4, 62, 98, 142; EEC issue, 37, 39, 62, 69, 72, 78-85, 142, 169, Shadow Cabinet resignations, 83-4; Far Left and entryism, 71, 104-8, 113, 160-1, Underhill Report, 106-7, 160, 186, investigation into, 186; future of, 199-203; historic decline, 92-5, 98, 101-4, 108-9, 136-7, 199-201; House of Lords Reform, 62, 120, 122, 136; incomes policy, 63-6, 71-2, 74-6; leaders and Prime Ministers, Keir Hardie, 180 (*see also* **Gaitskell**, Hugh, **Wilson**, Harold, **Callaghan**, James, **Foot**, Michael); leadership elections, 48, 61, 118, 138-9; deputy leadership elections, 83, 161-2, 170, 185-6; left-wing campaign, 36, 50, 51, 70-1, 104, 117-21, 122-7, 142-4, 158-9, 160-5, 184, 196, 199; modernisation of (Clause 4 controversy), 30, 39-44, 46, 53-5, 61, 67-8, 69, 78, 86, 100-1, 200-2; National Executive Committee, 36, 41, 44, 46, 49, 64, 67, 69, 70, 80, 82, 88, 106, 108, 120, 123, 136, 140, 142, 144, 186; origins, traditions and composition, 6, 27-30, 32-4, 100-4, 153, 200, 202 party democracy issue, 27-8, 37, 47-50, 52-4, 69-70, 117-21, 141, 196, control of manifesto, 117, 119, 122, 134, 142, 144, electoral procedure, 48, 69-70, 117, 119-20, 142, reselection issue, 119, 126-7, 141-2, 162; social reforms, 68, 124; right wing, 54, 109-10, 118, 119, 120, 125-6, 138, 140-2, 162, 185, 199, Manifesto, 110, 113, 127, Solidarity, 159-60, SDA (Social Democratic Alliance), 110-1, 133 (*see also* **CDS**, **CLV**); TU legislation, 62, 63-4, 66-8, 71-2, 73, 74

LRC (Labour Representation Council), 32, 153, 180, 185 (*see also* **Labour Party**, origins)

Lib-Lab Pact, 70, 126, 176

Liberal Party, assemblies, Blackpool 1980, 175, Llandudno 1981, 174-5; attitude to Alliance, 174-7; electoral results, 6, 93, 94, 95, 96; leaders, Grimond, Jo, 180, 183, Steel, David, 14, 20, 23-4, 133, 167, 174-6, 177, 179, 182, 194, 204; Pincham, Roger, 127-8, 176 (*see also* **SDP Alliance**)

Lindley, Clive, 2, 127-8, 132, 147, 175

Livingstone, Ken, 164

222

Magee, Brian, 29, 30, 51

Manifesto Group, *see* Labour Party, right wing

Marquand, David, 111, 133, 147, 166, 176, 201

Militant Tendency, *see* Labour Party, Far Left

National Front, *see* Political Parties, rise of minority parties

Nationalist Parties, *see* Political Parties, rise of minority parties

Owen, David, and socialism, 29, 44; in Labour Party, 23, 84, 136, 139, 146; and CLV, 128, 134-5; and SDP, 5, 12, 23, 119, 153, 154, 168; and Liberals, 175, 176

Pickstock, Frank, *see* CDS

Political Parties, rise of minority parties, 9, 94-8; Oswald Mosley's New Party, 6; (*see also* Conservative, Labour and Liberal Parties)

PR (Proportional Representation), *see* Electoral System, case for reform, and SDP, electoral reform

Radical Centre for Democratic Studies in Industry and Society, 132-3

Rank & File Mobilising Committee, *see* Labour Party, left-wing campaign

Rodgers, Bill, in Labour Government, 23; and CDS, 45, 51-5; and CLV, 110, 127-9, 134-5; formation of SDP, 5, 12, 137, 139, 144-5, 146, 147, 153-4, Abertillery speech, 129-30; and SDP, 176, 178, 179, 205

Scottish Nationalists, *see* Political Parties, rise of minority parties

SDP (Social Democratic Party), conferences: 13, 154, 187; creation and early days, 5-9, 10, 152-5, 155-7, open letter to *Guardian*, 139, Limehouse Declaration, 6, 8, 16-9, 119, 120, 151-3, 176; economic policy, 18, 152, 169, 187; electoral reform, 16-7, 130-1, 169, 182, 197; foreign policy, 18-9, 152, 169, 187; leadership, 20-4, 187, 204; membership, 10-2, 187; opinion poll ratings, 14, 155; parliamentary party, 12-3; reform of political structure, 15, 16, 130-1, 151-2; social policy, 18, 187; Sofer, Anne, 156

SDP/Liberal Alliance,
174-82; election results,
183-4, 192; forerunners,
180-2; 'A Fresh Start for
Britain', 176; future of,
182, 192-5, 197, 204-6;
leadership question, 204;
need for, 173, 174, 176;
policies, 14; preceding
moves, 127-8, 174-6;
selection of candidates,
177-80

Shore, Peter, *see* **Labour
Party**, right wing

Socialism, British, 27-31,
33; Brockway, Fenner, 2,
29, 108; Crosland,
Anthony and *The Future
of Socialism*, 30, 31, 34,
39, 129

Solidarity (Labour
Solidarity Campaign), *see*
Labour Party, right wing

S P D
(Sozialdemokratische
Partei Deutschlands), 21,
43-4, 100

Steel, David, *see* **Liberal
Party**

Taverne, Dick, 2; and
Labour Party, 72, 84, 111,
126, 127, 160; CDS, 51-2;
CSD, 77, 86-90, 95, 156;
and SDP, 55, 133, 137-8,
147, 167

Thatcher, Margaret, *see*
Conservative Party,
leaders

Trade Unions, AEU, 47,
65; GMWU, 36; NUM, 36,
74, 89; NUPE, 71;
TGWU, 35, 36, 47, 53, 63,
65, 71, 185

Trade Union Leaders,
Chapple, Frank, 144;
Cousins, Frank, 47, 49,
53, 63, 65; Deakin,
Arthur, 36; Fisher, Alan,
71; Gormley, Joe, 80;
Jones, Jack, 65, 71, 75,
90, 125, 126; Scanlon,
Hugh, 65, 71, 125

Trade Unions, role and
activities, 47, 49, 63-4,
65-6, 69, 70, 71-3, 74, 75-6,
89, 95, 123-5

Tribune Group, 51, 69-70,
83, 87, 107-8, 120, 161,
163; Neil Kinnock, 131,
158, 163, 167, 199 (*see
also* **Labour Party**, left-
wing campaign)

Trotskyists, *see* **Labour
Party**, Far Left

Underhill Report, *see*
Labour Party, Far Left

Welsh Nationalists, *see*
Political Parties, rise of
minority parties

Williams, Shirley, and
socialism, 101; in Labour
Party, 12, 18, 81, 142,
attitude to Left, 51, 105,
108, 122, 144, 160; and
CLV, 110, 128, 134-5,

144-5; run-up to SDP, 5, 133-4, 136, 137, 138, 139, 146; in SDP, 18, 153-4, 157, 167, 168, 172; and Liberals, 176, 177, 178; leadership, 21-3; and Crosby, 178, 183

Wilson, Harold, and socialism, 28, 29, 41, 167; and leadership, 48, 53; as leader, 21, 36, 59-75, 87, 99, 100, 118; attitude to Left Wing, 105

OTHER BOOKS
ON
POLITICS

Political Parties in Europe

By Theo Stammen
With a foreword by Dick Taverne QC

Limp cover: £10.95

'This work is timely and informative ... it presents a wealth of primary source material ... It is also characterised by an unusual degree of coherence and rigour in its format and analytical content.' (*Choice*, March 1981)

The Meaning of Social Democracy and Other Essays

Edited by John Martin

Publication date: June, 1982
Paperback: £2.50

Available from John Martin Publishing Limited
15 King Street, Covent Garden, London WC2

D7